The Environmental Impact Statement Process and Environmental Law

Second Edition

7/25/2000

George:

I hope you enjoy the improved version, with my best personal and professional regards.

Emmett

Emmett B. Moore, Ph.D.

Adjunct Professor of Environmental Science
Washington State University

 **Battelle Press**

Columbus • Richland

Library of Congress Cataloging-in-Publication Data

Moore, Emmett Burris, 1929–
    The environmental impact statement process and environmental law /
Emmett B. Moore—2nd ed.
        p. cm.
    Includes related legislation.
    Includes bibliographical references and index.
    ISBN 1-57477-092-6 (alk. paper)
    1.Environmental impact statements—United States. 2. Environmental
law—United States. I. United States. National Environmental Policy Act of
1969. II. Title.

TD194.55 .M66   2000
333.7'14'—dc21   00-026083

Printed in the United States of America

Battelle Press
505 King Avenue
Columbus, Ohio 43201, USA
1-614-424-6393 or 1-800-451-3543
Fax: 1-614-424-3819
E-mail: press@battelle.org
Home page: http://www.battelle.org/bookstore

Preface

This second edition of *The Environmental Impact Statement Process and Environmental Law* has been expanded to include improved chapters on environmental assessment and risk assessment, a brief section on internet sources, a brief conclusion, and other improvements to bring the text up to date for the year 2000. The first edition was an outgrowth of my experience as director of power plant siting (and transmission line routing) for the State of Minnesota Environmental Quality Board, as a staff scientist at the Pacific Northwest National Laboratory, and as an adjunct professor of environmental science at Washington State University. This experience included managing the Minnesota power plant siting and transmission line routing processes; managing the preparation of Minnesota environmental impact statements on power plants and transmission lines; preparing and managing the preparation of federal environmental assessments and environmental impact statements at the Pacific Northwest National Laboratory; and teaching environmental law, environmental assessment, and hazardous waste management at Washington State University.

My first experience with the National Environmental Policy Act occurred not at the national level but at the state level when I argued for recognition of the Minnesota transmission line routing process as the functional equivalent of the Minnesota environmental impact statement (EIS) process. I was soundly thrashed by my environmental colleagues in state government, and we proceeded to carry out wasteful, duplicative, and unnecessary processes. In the intervening 20 years, matters have improved with respect to environmental documentation at all levels of government (see the sections on functional equivalence and categorical exclusions), but further improvements are still possible. Some of these potential improvements are discussed in various places in the book.

This book is intended for a one quarter or one semester environmental science course at the upper division or graduate level on environmental assessment with emphasis on the preparation of federal environmental impact statements. The book includes a brief introduction to environmental law, because it is not possible to prepare an adequate EIS without a substantial knowledge of environmental law. Although short, the book contains enough material for the stated purpose. For the convenience of the reader, citations to the United States Code (federal law) and the Code of Federal Regulations (federal regulations) are presented throughout the book. The National Environmental Policy Act and its implementing regulations are reprinted as appendices. I expect the book to be useful both to environmental science students and to professionals in the field.

I dedicate this book to my wife, Diane, and to our children, Karen and Robin, who have been great joys to me throughout my environmental science career.

Emmett B. Moore

Table of Contents

Table of Contents (Continued)

Table of Contents (Continued)

Table of Contents (Continued)

Acronyms

AEA	Atomic Energy Act
AEC	Atomic Energy Commission
APA	Administrative Procedure Act
ARAR	applicable or relevant and appropriate requirement
BACT	best available control technology
BOD	biological oxygen demand
CAA	Clean Air Act
CEQ	Council on Environmental Quality
CERCLA	Comprehensive Environmental Response, Compensation, and Liability Act
CFR	*Code of Federal Regulations*
COE	U.S. Army Corps of Engineers
CWA	Clean Water Act
CX	categorical exclusion
DOA	U.S. Department of Agriculture
DOE	U.S. Department of Energy
DOI	U.S. Department of the Interior
DOT	U.S. Department of Transportation
EA	environmental assessment
EIS	environmental impact statement
EPA	U.S. Environmental Protection Agency
ESA	Endangered Species Act
FFCA	Federal Facilities Compliance Act
FONSI	finding of no significant impact
FR	*Federal Register*
FWPCA	Federal Water Pollution Control Act
HSWA	Hazardous and Solid Waste Amendments (to RCRA)
IRIS	Integrated Risk Information System
LLRWPA	Low-Level Radioactive Waste Policy Act
MACT	maximum achievable control technology
MCL	maximum contaminant levels
MCLG	maximum contaminant level goal
NAAQS	National Ambient Air Quality Standards
NCP	National Contingency Plan
NEPA	National Environmental Policy Act
NESHAP	National Emission Standards for Hazardous Air Pollutants
NHPA	National Historic Preservation Act
NOA	notice of availability
NOI	notice of intent
NPDES	National Pollutant Discharge Elimination System
NPL	National Priorities List
NRDA	natural resource damage assessment
NRC	U.S. Nuclear Regulatory Commission
NSC	National Safety Council
NSPS	new source performance standards
NWPA	Nuclear Waste Policy Act

Acronyms (Continued)

OPA	Oil Pollution Act
PCB	polychlorinated biphenyls
POTW	publicly owned treatment works
PSD	prevention of significant deterioration
RACT	reasonably available control technology
RCRA	Resource Conservation and Recovery Act
RD/RA	remedial design/remedial action
RI/FS	remedial investigation/feasibility study
ROD	record of decision
SARA	Superfund Amendments and Reauthorization Act
SDWA	Safe Drinking Water Act
SEPA	state environmental policy act
SHPO	state historic preservation officer
SIP	state implementation plans
SS	suspended solids
TCLP	toxicity characteristic leaching procedure
TSCA	Toxic Substances Control Act
TSD	treatment, storage, and/or disposal
UIC	underground injection control
USC	*United States Code*
UST	underground storage tank

Chapter 1 — Introduction to the National Environmental Policy Act

Before 1970, it was environmental science that drove environmental law. That is to say, it was scientific knowledge that demonstrated the necessity for laws to protect the environment (beyond obvious situations such as grossly contaminated water). Examples include knowledge about the bioaccumulation of pesticides as detailed in Rachel Carson's book *Silent Spring,*[1] knowledge about the impacts of siting large energy facilities, and knowledge about smog and its impacts in Los Angeles. Since 1970, many new environmental laws have been passed and older environmental laws have been substantially amended (see Figure 1). Now at the turn of the century the situation is reversed, it is environmental law that drives environmental science. Environmental law and environmental regulations mandate what environmental scientists must do with respect to monitoring air quality, monitoring water quality, limiting emissions to the atmosphere, limiting effluents to bodies of water, protecting endangered species, protecting wetlands, protecting prime farmland, protecting cultural resources, managing hazardous wastes, and cleaning up abandoned waste sites. These activities and the associated environmental laws now provide a directory of what must be included in an environmental impact statement (EIS).

1970 is a convenient reference date because the National Environmental Policy Act (NEPA) was passed in 1969 and signed by President Nixon on January 1, 1970, the U.S. Environmental Protection Agency (EPA) was established in 1970, and the bulk of the existing environmental law was passed after 1970. NEPA, of course, created the requirement that federal agencies prepare EISs.

The Legal Framework of NEPA (and Other Environmental Laws)

The legal framework of federal environmental law begins with the Constitution of the United States, which is the fundamental legal document in this country. The framework includes the Congress, state legislatures, federal agencies, state agencies, and the federal judiciary (Figure 2). State legislatures and agencies are included because the Congress has authorized state enforcement of certain federal environmental laws either directly or by delegation, usually from the EPA.

U.S. Constitution

The U.S. Constitution is a brief document that created a federal government of rather limited authority (Article I) in three branches: executive, legislative, and judicial. The legislative branch consists of the two houses of Congress which pass laws. The executive branch consists of the President, the federal cabinet, and the federal executive agencies. The President and the federal agencies carry out and enforce federal laws. The President also recommends legislation to Congress and approves or vetoes Congressional legislation. Federal agencies promulgate federal regulations. The judicial branch consists of the federal courts which adjudicate disputes under federal law involving the federal government, adjudicate disputes between and among states, interpret federal law and in so doing sometimes create case law, and decide on the constitutionality of federal laws.

	Acronym	1940	1950	1960	1970	1980	1990	2000
State Drinking Water Act Amendments	SDWAA							•
Federal Facilities Compliance Act	FFCA						•	
Clean Air Act Amendments	CAAA						•	
Pollution Prevention Act	PPA						•	
Oil Pollution Act	OPA						•	
Low-Level Radioactive Waste Policy Act	LLRWPA					•		
Superfund Amendments and Reauthorization Act	SARA					•		
Hazardous and Solid Waste Amendments (to RCRA)	HSWA					•		
Nuclear Waste Policy Act	NWPA					•		
Comprehensive Environmental Response, Compensation, and Liability Act	CERCLA					•		
Clean Water Act	CWA				•			
Resource Conservation and Recovery Act	RCRA				•			
Toxic Substances Control Act	TSCA				•			
Safe Drinking Water Act	SDWA				•			
Hazardous Materials Transportation Act	HMTA				•			
Endangered Species Act	ESA				•			
Federal Water Pollution Control Act	FWPCA				•			
Noise Control Act	NCA				•			
Clean Air Act	CAA				•			
National Environmental Policy Act	NEPA				•			
Solid Waste Disposal Act	SWDA			•				
National Historic Preservation Act	NHPA			•				
Atomic Energy Act	AEA		•					
Federal Water Pollution Control Act	FWPCA	•						

Figure 1. Partial list of federal environmental laws passed by the U.S. Congress since 1948. While some environmental laws were passed before 1948, the bulk of the environmental activity by Congress has occurred since 1948.

No specific authority is given by the Constitution to Congress to pass environmental laws. However, students of government suggest that the commerce clause (Article I, Section 8,3), the power to provide for the general welfare (Article I, Section 8,1), and/ or the power to tax and spend (Article I, Section 8,1) provide adequate justification for the Congress to pass environmental laws. The powers of the federal government were intended to be those specifically stated in the Constitution, with the rest reserved to the states, according to Amendment X, which states that, "The powers not delegated to the United States by the constitution, nor prohibited by it to the states, are reserved to the

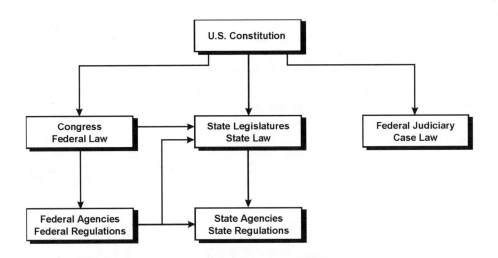

Figure 2. Relationship among the U.S. Constitution, federal laws and regulations, state laws and regulations, and federal case law.

states respectively, or to the people." Nevertheless, the Congress has found it in the public interest to provide a full set of environmental laws that are complemented, or even duplicated, by state law.

Two clauses in the constitution are of particular importance in environmental law although they are not of special relevance to NEPA. These are the commerce clause and the due process clause. The commerce clause appears in Article I, Section 8,3 and states that: "The Congress shall have the power to regulate commerce . . . among the several states." The importance of the commerce clause to environmental law includes the fact that the states do not have the authority to regulate the importation of hazardous or radioactive wastes without the specific permission of Congress.

The due process clauses appear in Amendment V and Amendment XIV, Section 1. Amendment V, the federal due process clause defines the "taking" issue and states that: "No person shall . . . be deprived of life, liberty, or property, without due process of law; nor shall private property be taken for public use without just compensation;" and Amendment XIV, Section 1 states that: ". . . nor shall any state deprive any person of life, liberty, or property without due process of the law." The importance of the due process clauses in environmental law is that private property may not be taken by the government without just compensation, and courts have recently ruled that the denial of an environmental permit may constitute a taking subject to compensation.

Federal Law

Article I, Section 1 of the Constitution states that, "All legislative powers herein granted shall be vested in a Congress of the United States, which shall consist of a Senate and House of Representatives." Congress passes federal laws, and the President signs or vetoes each law. In addition the Congress may give agencies the authority to promulgate regulations to implement the law.

Federal Regulations

Federal regulations have the full force and effect of federal law. However, federal regulations (usually) are not made by Congress, but are made by agencies of the executive branch such as the Council on Environmental Quality (CEQ), the EPA, the Department of the Interior (DOI), the Department of Agriculture (DOA), the Department of Energy (DOE), etc. This must be done in accordance with the Administrative Procedure Act (APA) (5 USC 551 et seq.). This usually involves publication of a draft of the proposed regulations in the *Federal Register* (FR), frequently after a long intra- and interagency review period; solicitation of comments; conduct of a public hearing; preparation (sometimes) of an environmental assessment (EA) or an EIS; publication of the final regulations in the FR; and codification in the *Code of Federal Regulations* (CFR). Sometimes Congress intrudes in this rulemaking process and effectively preempts an agency's regulatory function by inserting regulatory language directly into federal laws. The list of 189 toxic air pollutants in the Clean Air Act Amendments of 1990 is a good example of this.

State Law

State laws are passed by state legislatures. The state legislatures can pass anything not specifically reserved to the federal government or anything not prevented by the federal or state constitution (Amendment X). Frequently, the statement is made that health, safety, and welfare matters are the province of the states. State legislatures can also act on any matter specifically delegated by Congress, such as waivers of sovereign immunity that allow the states to regulate federal facilities. In general, however, the federal government cannot force states to pass laws they don't want to pass.

State Regulations

State regulations are usually promulgated by state agencies according to a state administrative procedure act. In Washington, a draft is published in the *Washington State Register*, a comment period is held usually with a hearing, the final regulations are published in the *Washington State Register*, and then the regulations are codified in the *Washington Administrative Code*.

State Environmental Policy Acts

Many states have a state environmental policy act (SEPA), equivalent to NEPA, which applies to state agencies. In some of those states there is now substantial cooperation between the state and the federal government in the matter of the preparation of environmental documents. See "Lead and Joint Agencies for the Preparation of an EIS" in Chapter 4. Frequently, an adequate federal EIS will substitute for a state EIS.

Federal Court Structure

The federal courts consist of the district courts (usually one or more in each state), the circuit courts of appeal, and the Supreme Court. The district courts are courts of original jurisdiction in matters involving federal law; the circuit courts are usually courts of appeal, although in some cases they have original jurisdiction; and the Supreme Court is almost always a court of appeal. The Supreme Court has original jurisdiction in cases between states or between the U.S. and a state, and in a few other situations. The Supreme Court decides what cases it will hear and therefore may effectively affirm a circuit court's decision by refusing to hear an appeal.

Case Law

Federal and state courts decide disputes, and in some situations it is necessary for the court to interpret a law in deciding the dispute. When this occurs, the interpretation is called "case law." This case law then applies to other cases within the jurisdiction of the deciding court and may be used as a precedent in other jurisdictions. The Congress or legislature may then revise the statutory law to negate the case law. A lot of case law exists with respect to NEPA, some of which is discussed in the following chapters.

Citations

Federal laws are codified in the *United States Code* (USC) and federal regulations are codified in the CFR. State laws are codified in compilations of state statutes that have different names in different states (Washington State laws appear in the *Revised Code of Washington*). State regulations appear in compilations of state regulations, again with different names in different states (Washington State regulations appear in the *Washington Administrative Code*). Official notices of the federal government appear in the FR, and official notices of states usually appear in a similar publication (notices of Washington State agencies appear in the *Washington State Register*). Sample citations are 42 USC 4321 et seq., 40 CFR 1500, and 56 FR 33050. For the convenience of the reader, citations to federal law and federal regulations are presented in the text throughout this book.

Information on the Internet

Information on laws, regulations, and environmental matters may be obtained from various agencies and organizations through their Internet sites. For example, the *United States Code*, the *Code of Federal Regulations*, and the *Federal Register* can be accessed through the Government Printing Office at www.access.gpo.gov. The same documents, as well as case law, can be found at www.findlaw.com. Agency and organization addresses of interest include:

Council on Environmental Quality (CEQ)	www.whitehouse.gov/CEQ
Department of Agriculture (DOA)	www.usda.gov
Department of Commerce (DOC)	www.doc.gov
Department of Defense (DOD)	www.defenselink.mil
Department of Energy (DOE)	www.doe.gov
Environmental Protection Agency (EPA)	www.epa.gov
Government Printing Office (GPO)	www.access.gpo.gov
National Academy of Sciences	www.nas.edu
National Marine Fisheries Service (NMFS)	www.nmfs.gov
National Safety Council (NSC)	www.nsc.org
U.S. Fish and Wildlife Service (FWS)	www.fws.gov
U.S. Nuclear Regulatory Commission (NRC)	www.nrc.gov

Dose-response information may be found in the Integrated Risk Information System (IRIS) section of the EPA site. Lists of published EISs and contact persons may be found on the CEQ site. Accident statistics may be obtained from the NSC site. Lists of threatened or endangered species may be found on the FWS and NMFS sites. Information on models useful in pathway analyses may be found on the EPA site.

Overview of NEPA and the NEPA Process (42 USC 4321-4347)

NEPA[2] was passed by Congress in late 1969 and signed by President Nixon on January 1, 1970. NEPA laid the foundation for the NEPA process, created the CEQ, and ushered in the environmental era for the federal government. NEPA speaks to agencies of the federal government and is regarded by many persons as the cornerstone of federal public environmental policy.

A few environmental laws were passed before 1970, such as the Clean Air Act (CAA) which was passed in 1963; but most were passed later, including the Safe Drinking Water Act (SDWA) in 1974; the Clean Water Act (CWA) in 1977; the Resource Conservation and Recovery Act (RCRA) in 1976; the Comprehensive Environmental Response, Compensation, and Liability Act (CERCLA) in 1982; the Hazardous and Solid Waste Amendments (HSWA) to RCRA in 1984; and the Superfund Amendments and Reauthorization Act (SARA) in 1986 (see Figure 1). These environmental laws are closely linked to the NEPA process and to the content of the EIS.

Title I of NEPA establishes a national environmental policy, and Title II creates the CEQ. Section 102(2)(C) of NEPA states that "all agencies of the Federal Government shall . . . include in every recommendation or report on proposals for legislation and other major Federal actions significantly affecting the quality of the human environment, a detailed statement by the responsible official on—(i) the environmental impact of the proposed action, (ii) any adverse environmental effects which cannot be avoided should the proposal be implemented, (iii) alternatives to the proposed action, (iv) the relationship between the local short-term uses of man's environment and the maintenance and enhancement of long-term productivity, and (v) any irreversible and irretrievable commitments of resources which would be involved in the proposed action should it be implemented." The major import of this section is that federal agencies are directed to prepare EISs for any major federal action significantly affecting the quality of the human environment. Furthermore, the EIS is to contain discussions of items (i) through (v). NEPA applies to federal agencies, that is to say, federal agencies, not others, prepare EISs. Section 102(2)(C) is the heart of NEPA and provides the threshold for the preparation of an EIS.

CEQ

Title II of NEPA establishes the CEQ (chairman and two members). The chairman reports directly to the President of the United States. The CEQ created the NEPA process from Title I of NEPA. CEQ promulgates regulations, prepares an annual Environmental Quality Report, reviews environmental programs of federal agencies, conducts investigations related to the quality of the environment, mediates environmental impact disputes between federal agencies, and submits recommendations to the President in cases where the dispute cannot be resolved. EPA is often one of these federal agencies, and an EPA referral to the CEQ is usually based on an unsatisfactory EIS (CAA Section 309, 40 CFR 1504). The NEPA process includes the EIS process. An interesting facet of NEPA is that NEPA does not give CEQ explicit authority to promulgate regulations. However, two executive orders confer this authority on the CEQ (EO 11514 Nixon, EO 11991 Carter).

CEQ Regulations (40 CFR 1500-1508)

The CEQ regulations in 40 CFR 1500-1508[3] implement NEPA and provide rules for the preparation of EISs. The rules describe the kinds of actions for which an EIS must be prepared, prescribe the format and content of an EIS, describe other reviews and analyses that may or must be included in the EIS, and provide for procedural and public participation matters attendant to the EIS process (in total often called the NEPA or, more narrowly, the EIS process). The regulations also provide for categorical exclusions (CXs) and for the preparation of EAs. The last major revision of the CEQ regulations was in 1978. In order to understand fully the NEPA process and the EIS process, one must be familiar with all of 40 CFR 1500-1508. Therefore, the student should read and become familiar with all of 40 CFR 1500-1508.

This book is about NEPA, the NEPA process, and the EIS process. NEPA, of course, is the law that authorizes the NEPA process. The NEPA process itself is described in the CEQ regulations in 40 CFR 1500-1508 and includes the full range of activities that might be undertaken by a federal agency in evaluating the environmental impacts of a proposed action. These activities include the determination of a categorical exclusion, the preparation of an EA, and/or the preparation of an EIS. The EIS process includes the preparation of the EIS and all of the procedural and public participation activities that accompany the preparation of the EIS. This book also includes a discussion of environmental law because an understanding of environmental law is important to understanding many of the analyses that must be carried out in preparing an EIS. The reader is referred to Thomas F. P. Sullivan et al.[4] for a more legalistic discussion of environmental law.

REFERENCES

(1)   Rachel Carson, *Silent Spring*, Houghton-Mifflin, Boston, 1972.

(2)   The National Environmental Policy Act, 42 USC 4321-4347.

(3)   Council on Environmental Quality Regulations Implementing NEPA, 40 CFR 1500-1508.

(4)   Thomas F. P. Sullivan, et al. *Environmental Law Handbook*, Fifteenth Edition, Government Institutes, 1999.

Before discussing the NEPA process, it is appropriate to consider the various documents that could be products of the NEPA process at one stage or another. An environmental document is defined in 40 CFR 1508.1 as an EA, EIS, finding of no significant impact (FONSI), or notice of intent (NOI). Two other documents are not environmental documents under the CEQ definition, but are discussed here because they are an integral part of the NEPA process. These are the categorical exclusion (CX) and the record of decision (ROD). A CX is not necessarily a document; but, when an agency decides that an action is covered by a CX, it usually prepares some documentation to justify that decision. The CX and ROD, although not official environmental documents, are discussed here for completeness. The relationship among the various documents is shown in Figure 3.

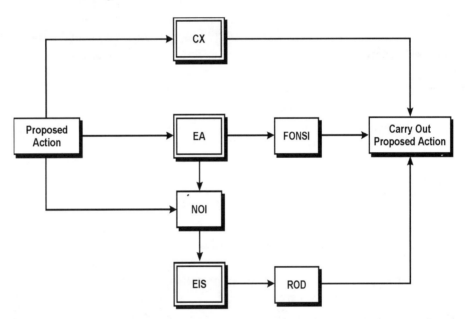

Figure 3. NEPA flow chart. Unless a proposed action qualifies for a CX, then either an EA or an EIS must be prepared by the proposing federal agency. If an EA is prepared, then a FONSI will allow the agency to proceed with its proposed action. Otherwise, a NOI must be published in the _Federal Register_ and an EIS prepared, the end result of which is a ROD that will allow the agency to proceed. The decision in the ROD may not necessarily be the agency's proposed action.

Categorical Exclusion (40 CFR 1500.5, 1507.3(b)(2), and 1508.4)

A CX refers to an action that does not require either an EA or an EIS, i.e., an action that does not individually or cumulatively have a significant effect on the environment. Actions that qualify for a CX must meet criteria in an agency's procedures and are usually listed in an agency's procedures, i.e., have been approved by the CEQ. See, for example Subpart D of the U.S. Department of Energy regulations in 10 CFR 1021. There is room for agencies to improve their compliance with NEPA by carefully expanding their lists of actions that qualify for a categorical exclusion. Serious thought could significantly reduce the number of unnecessary EAs that are prepared, as well as the expense to the taxpayer.

Environmental Assessment
(40 CFR 1508.9)

"Environmental assessment [EA]: (a) Means a concise public document for which a Federal agency is responsible that serves to: (1) Briefly provide sufficient evidence and analysis for determining whether to prepare an environmental impact statement or a finding of no significant impact, (2) Aid an agency's compliance with the Act when no environmental impact statement is necessary, or (3) Facilitate preparation of a statement [EIS] when one is necessary. (b) Shall include brief discussions of the need for the proposal, of alternatives as required by section 102(2)(E), of the environmental impacts of the proposed action and alternatives, and a listing of agencies and persons consulted." The end product of an EA is a FONSI, a decision to prepare an EIS, i.e., a notice of intent, or no action. No action results when an agency simply decides to abandon a project without completing the environmental paperwork. The CEQ regulations direct agencies to involve environmental agencies, applicants, and the public in the preparation of EAs, to the extent practicable (40 CFR 1501.4(b)).

Finding of No Significant Impact
(40 CFR 1508.13)

"Finding of no significant impact [FONSI] means a document by a Federal agency briefly presenting the reasons why an action, not otherwise excluded (40 CFR 1508.4), will not have a significant effect on the human environment and for which an environmental impact statement therefore will not be prepared. It shall include the environmental assessment or a summary of it and shall note any other environmental documents related to it (40 CFR 1501.7(a)(5)). If the assessment is included, the finding need not repeat any of the discussion in the assessment but may incorporate it by reference." A FONSI is one of the three possible outcomes of an EA.

Notice of Intent
(40 CFR 1508.22)

"Notice of intent [NOI] means a notice that an environmental impact statement will be prepared and considered. The notice shall briefly: (a) Describe the proposed action and possible alternatives. (b) Describe the agency's proposed scoping process including whether, when, and where any scoping meeting will be held. (c) State the name and address of a person within the agency who can answer questions about the proposed action and the environmental impact statement." The NOI can also include a list of the impacts expected to be discussed in the EIS. The NOI should be published in the *Federal Register.*

The NOI may be the end product of an EA or the result of an agency's decision to prepare an EIS without having prepared an EA. Normally the agency's procedures that list actions qualifying for a CX will also list actions normally requiring an EA or an EIS.

Environmental Impact Statement (40 CFR 1508.11)

"Environmental impact statement [EIS] means a detailed written statement as required by section 102(2)(C) of the Act" (NEPA). The test is any "major federal action significantly affecting the quality of the human environment." In fact, this is the threshold for any action under NEPA. Any lesser action does not require any environmental documentation. The end product of an EIS is a record of decision, although sometimes the process is not completed and "no action" becomes the end product.

Record of Decision (40 CFR 1501.2(b) and 1505.2)

The ROD is published in the *Federal Register* after the publication of the final EIS. It records the agency's decision and may include factors other than the environmental impacts considered in the EIS, for example, economic and technical considerations and statutory missions. Thus, the ROD may not be the agency's proposed action or its environmentally preferred alternative if other considerations outweigh environmental considerations. (See Chapter 4, The Record of Decision).

At the outset, it must be remembered that NEPA and the CEQ regulations apply to federal agencies. When a federal agency proposes an action, the agency must examine that action in order to determine what level of environmental evaluation is appropriate for the action. With a few exceptions, any "major federal action significantly affecting the quality of the human environment" will require the agency to prepare an EIS. It is interesting to note that if the proposed action is not a major federal action significantly affecting the quality of the human environment, then the agency need do nothing. Nothing more is required under NEPA. However, if the agency is in doubt as to whether or not an EIS must be prepared, then the agency must prepare an EA. Also, an agency will usually list in its procedures actions that are categorically excluded from the necessity of preparing either an EA or an EIS. What constitutes a categorically excluded action should be predetermined, listed in the agency's procedures, and approved by the CEQ. Actions that do not require an EIS, but for which the agency wishes to prepare an EA, should also be listed in the agency's procedures.

Requirements Triggering the Preparation of an EA (40 CFR 1501.3, 1507.3(b)(2), and 1508.9)

A federal agency must prepare an EA whenever one is required under the agency's procedures, or whenever uncertainty exists as to whether or not to prepare an EIS. An agency may prepare an EA to aid the agency in its compliance with NEPA or to facilitate preparation of an EIS when one is necessary. The table of contents of an EA is quite simple and is presented in Chapter 2 under "Environmental Assessment (3)(b)." The end result of an EA is a FONSI, a decision to prepare an EIS, or no action.

As a practical matter, few agencies prepare an EA because of doubt as to whether or not an EIS is required. More frequently than not, an agency will prepare an EA when the agency wishes to avoid preparing an EIS. Usually this works, but it didn't for the Department of Energy when it prepared an EA on the restart of the K Reactor at Savannah River, South Carolina, in the late 1980s. The DOE was sued, the DOE lost, and the DOE had to prepare an EIS, which it was able to do in a short period of time because it already had an EA in hand. All of this turned out to be money wasted, however, because the DOE never effectively restarted the reactor.

Requirements Triggering the Preparation of an EIS (40 CFR 1501.4 and 1507.3(b)(2))

The criteria (above) in the CEQ regulations that trigger the preparation of an EA are rather short and simple. On the other hand, the criteria that trigger the preparation of on EIS are rather extensive. These criteria are the components of the phrase: "a major federal action significantly affecting the quality of the human environment" (40 CFR 1502.3). Although the CEQ regulations provide lengthy definitions for each component, some observers say the criteria are vague and/or indefinite. This may be because the definitions of the components tend only to list items to be considered in making the decision, rather than provide definite guidelines as to whether or not an EIS should be prepared. The definitions of each component of the phrase "major federal action significantly affecting the quality of the human environment" are discussed below.

Major Federal Action
(40 CFR 1508.18)

"Major Federal action includes actions with effects that may be major and which are potentially subject to Federal control and responsibility. Major reinforces but does not have a meaning independent of significantly . . . (a) Actions include new and continuing activities, including projects and programs entirely or partly financed, assisted, conducted, regulated, or approved by federal agencies; new or revised agency rules, regulations, plans, policies, or procedures; and legislative proposals." Actions are most often focused on "Approval of specific projects, such as construction or management activities located in a defined geographic area. Projects include actions approved by [federal] permit or other regulatory decision as well as federal and federally assisted activities." Thus a private project funded by the federal government or requiring a federal permit may require an EIS. Substantial cost, substantial impacts, or substantial use of federally owned land will usually trigger preparation of an EIS.

"Major" sometimes has a small monetary value. For example, the U.S. District Court in Hawaii in 1991 decided that $5 million dollars constitutes a major federal action (Blue Ocean Preservation Society v. Energy Department). It should be noted, however, that other activities on the same project with substantial costs, federal involvement, and no environmental documentation had preceded the court case.

The matter of whether or not and how often a continuing activity may require a new EIS is not one that received much attention during the early days of NEPA, either from the agencies or the courts. Most agencies considered that activities in progress when NEPA was passed did not require new EISs. Now, there is some interest on the part of some environmental groups and agencies in providing environmental documentation for old activities and in updating existing environmental documents.

Significantly
(40 CFR 1508.27)

"Significantly" as used in NEPA requires consideration of both context and intensity. Context can include world, national, regional, and/or local effects, as well as short-term and long-term effects. "Intensity" refers to the severity of impact. Intensity may include 1) adverse or beneficial impacts; 2) intensity of the impact on human health or safety; 3) intensity of impact on the geographic area including cultural resources, parks, prime farmlands (a definition of prime farmland appears in the DOA regulations in 7 CFR 657), wetlands, wild and scenic rivers, and ecologically critical areas; 4) controversial impacts; 5) uncertain impacts; 6) establishment of a precedent; 7) relation to other acts which individually are insignificant, but together have cumulative impacts; 8) impacts on areas listed in or eligible for listing in the National Register of Historic

Places; 9) impacts on threatened or endangered species or on habitat critical under the Endangered Species Act; 10) whether or not action threatens a violation of federal, state, or local environmental law.

With respect to the definition of "significantly," there is no recipe, no prescription, no specific criteria, and no threshold. The definition only lists items to consider.

Affecting
(40 CFR 1508.3 and 1508.8)

"Affecting means will or may have an effect on." "Effects include (a) Direct effects, which are caused by the action and occur at the same time and place. (b) Indirect effects, which are caused by the action and are later in time or farther removed in distance, but are reasonably foreseeable. Indirect effects may include growth inducing effects and other effects related to induced changes in the pattern of land use, population density or growth rate, and related effects on air and water and other natural systems, including ecosystems." Effects include ecological, esthetic, historic, cultural, economic, social, and health effects, whether adverse, beneficial, direct, indirect, or cumulative.

The Quality of the Human Environment
(40 CFR 1508.14)

"Human environment" means "the natural and physical environment and the relationship of people with that environment." Economic or social effects are not intended by themselves to require preparation of an environmental impact statement. "When an environmental impact statement is prepared and economic or social and natural or physical environmental effects are interrelated, then the environmental impact statement will discuss all of these effects on the human environment."

Is Compliance with NEPA a Substantive or Procedural Matter?

In Vermont Yankee Nuclear Power Corp. v. NRDC in 1978, the Supreme Court noted that NEPA is a procedural requirement. An adequate EIS is one that meets CEQ regulations. An adequate EIS is all that is required to satisfy NEPA.[1] Restated; The acceptability of an EIS, either from the point of view of the rating by EPA or from the point of view of withstanding a court challenge, depends on whether or not the EIS meets the CEQ requirements. Corollary: Under NEPA, an agency must consider environmental impacts, but is not required to make decisions based solely on environmental impacts. The ROD may state a decision that is not consistent solely with environmental preservation. NEPA requires environmentally informed decisions, not necessarily environmentally correct decisions.

The Programmatic EIS
(40 CFR 1502.4 and 1502.20)

A programmatic EIS covers an entire program, and individual EISs for individual sites, facilities, or parts of the program are "tiered" from the programmatic EIS. The DC Circuit Court made this clear in Scientists' Institute for Public Information v. Atomic Energy Commission (AEC). In this suit over the liquid metal fast breeder reactor, the AEC said it would prepare an EIS for each facility at the time it was proposed. The DC Circuit Court directed the AEC to prepare a programmatic EIS. A programmatic EIS introduces the concept of tiering (40 CFR 1502.20). "Whenever a broad environmental impact statement has been prepared (such as a program or policy statement) and a subsequent statement or environmental assessment is then prepared on an action or policy (such as a site-specific action) the subsequent statement or environmental assessment need only summarize the issues discussed in the broader statement and incorporate discussions from the broader statement by reference and shall concentrate on the issues specific to the subsequent action."

As an example, the Department of Energy recently prepared a programmatic EIS on spent nuclear fuel[2] and then prepared a site-specific EIS tiered from the programmatic EIS on management of spent nuclear fuel at the Hanford Site.[3] The programmatic EIS covered all of DOE's spent nuclear fuel, examined existing sites at which to store the spent nuclear fuel, and examined transportation of the fuel from one DOE site to another according to each alternative. DOE's decision in the record of decision on the programmatic EIS was to leave at the Hanford Site most of the spent nuclear fuel already at Hanford. Accordingly, in the Hanford site-specific EIS, DOE examined various alternatives for the treatment and storage for up to 40 years of the DOE's spent nuclear fuel at Hanford.

The Supplemental EIS
(40 CFR 1502.9(c))

"Agencies: (1) Shall prepare supplements to either draft or final environmental impact statements if: (i) The agency makes substantial changes in the proposed action that are relevant to environmental concerns; or (ii) There are significant new circumstances or information relevant to environmental concerns and bearing on the proposed action or its impacts."

A supplementary EIS essentially restarts the EIS process, except that scoping is not required.

REFERENCES

(1) S. K. Fairfax, "A Disaster in the Environmental Movement," *Science* <u>199</u>, 743, 17 February 1978.

(2) *Department of Energy Programmatic Spent Nuclear Fuel Management and Idaho National Engineering Laboratory Environmental Restoration and Waste Management Programs Final Environmental Impact Statement*, U.S. Department of Energy, DOE/EIS-0203-F, April 1995.

(3) *Draft Environmental Impact Statement on Management of Spent Nuclear Fuel from the K Basins at the Hanford Site, Richland, Washington*, U.S. Department of Energy, DOE/EIS-0245D, October 1995; and Addendum, DOE/EIS-0245F, January 1996.

If a federal EIS is to be prepared, it must be prepared by a federal agency. An EA may be prepared by a contractor, and an EIS may be prepared by a contractor that does not have a conflict of interest; but the lead federal agency is, in both cases, responsible for the content of the EA or EIS. An EIS may also be prepared by a state agency under certain circumstances, but again, the lead federal agency is responsible (NEPA Sec. 102(D)).

Early case law made it clear that federal agencies must prepare an EIS for any major federal action significantly affecting the quality of the human environment. In Calvert Cliffs Coordinating Committee v. the AEC, the District of Columbia Circuit Court of Appeals ruled in 1971 that a federal agency (AEC in this case) must prepare an EIS for any major federal action significantly affecting the quality of the human environment, even though the agency's mandate might not specifically include environmental considerations.

Functional Equivalence

Since 1971, the Calvert Cliffs decision has been eroded both by Congress and by case law. For example, EPA does not now have to prepare an EIS for most of its regulatory actions. This is called functional equivalence. EPA's National Pollutant Discharge Elimination System (NPDES) permitting actions for existing sources are statutorily exempt from NEPA under the Clean Water Act (CWA Sec. 511(c)). No action under the CAA (Energy Supply and Environmental Coordination Act of 1974, 15 USC 791-798) is deemed to be a major federal action significantly affecting the quality of the human environment. Thus EPA actions under the CAA, as well as the actions of other federal agencies under the CAA, are exempt from NEPA. Case law exempts much of EPA's other regulatory activity from the preparation of an EIS under the Federal Insecticide, Fungicide, and Rodenticide Act; the Marine Protection, Research, and Sanctuaries Act; and RCRA. In Alabamians for a Clean Environment v. Thomas, the court for the Northern District of Alabama in 1987 held that the EPA's procedures for issuing RCRA permits are the functional equivalent of an EIS. The doctrine of functional equivalence is also being broadened under CERCLA and other environmental laws as well. For example, some cleanup actions under CERCLA, even though they appear to be major federal actions significantly affecting the quality of the human environment, are not accompanied by EISs. Also, the 9th Circuit Court of Appeals ruled in 1995 in Douglas County v. Bobbitt that an EIS need not accompany the designation of critical habitat under the Endangered Species Act; i.e., an EIS is not required for actions that preserve the environment.[1] Regulatory compliance activities of other federal agencies, even though directly related to the EPA activity, are in general not exempt from NEPA, except for actions under the CAA.

Early Preparation
(40 CFR 1500.5(f), 1501.2, 1502.2(g), and 1502.5)

An EIS must be prepared "early in the process." The EIS should be completed "early enough so that it can serve practically as an important contribution to the decision-making process and will not be used to rationalize or justify decisions already made."

This means that the project can be a long way from the final design stage at the time the EIS is prepared. However, if the EIS is too early and conditions change in the meantime, then a supplemental EIS may be required.

Lead and Joint Agencies
(40 CFR 1501.5)

The lead agency for the preparation of a federal EIS is the federal agency most responsible for the "major federal action..." It is the lead agency's job to prepare the EIS or to supervise its preparation. A federal agency may participate as a joint lead agency with state, local, or other federal agencies. For example the U.S. Bureau of Reclamation and the Washington Energy Facility Site Evaluation Council were joint lead agencies in the preparation of the draft EIS on the Creston Generating Station in north central Washington in 1981. Usually in the case of federal agencies only one federal agency is the lead agency, and other federal agencies are cooperating agencies.

Cooperating Agencies
(40 CFR 1501.6)

"Upon request of the lead agency, any other federal agency which has jurisdiction by law shall be a cooperating agency. In addition any other Federal agency which has special expertise with respect to any environmental issue, which should be addressed in the statement may be a cooperating agency upon request of the lead agency. An agency may request the lead agency to designate it a cooperating agency." A state or local agency may also be a cooperating agency (40 CFR 1508.5).

Preparing the EIS

The preparation of an EIS begins with the publication of the NOI and the conduct of the scoping process, it continues with the preparation and publication of the draft EIS, includes a period for public and agency comment on the draft EIS that may include public hearings, is followed by publication of the final EIS which contains the public and agency comments on the draft EIS and the lead agency's responses to those comments, and concludes with publication of the record of decision (Figure 4). These steps are discussed in more detail in the following sections.

Notice of Intent
(40 CFR 1501.7 and 1508.22)

The NOI (defined in Chapter 2) starts the scoping process. The lead agency must prepare an NOI and publish it in the *Federal Register*. The NOI must describe the proposed action and possible alternatives; describe the scoping process; and give the name, address, and telephone number of a responsible person within the agency who can answer questions about the proposed action and the EIS. The NOI should give the times, dates, and places of scoping meetings, if any; should list some (or all) of the impacts to be considered in the EIS; should invite agency and public comment on the scope of the EIS; and should present other appropriate background information.

Scoping and Scoping Meetings (40 CFR 1501.7, 1502.2(e), and 1508.25)

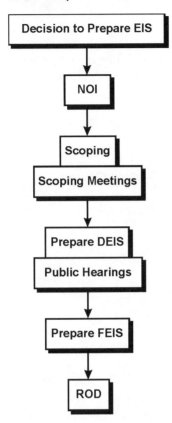

Figure 4. EIS flow chart. After a federal agency decides to prepare an EIS, it publishes an NOI in the *Federal Register*, undertakes a public scoping process, prepares the draft EIS, conducts public hearings on the draft EIS, prepares the final EIS, and publishes its ROD in the *Federal Register*.

As part of scoping, the lead agency must invite the participation of interested organizations, agencies, tribes, and persons; must determine the scope of the EIS, which includes identifying significant issues that are to be analyzed in depth and identifying issues that are not significant or have already been analyzed in other EAs or EISs; and must identify environmental review and consultation requirements. The purpose of scoping is to determine the range of actions, alternatives, and impacts to be considered in the EIS. The lead agency must consider unconnected (single) actions, connected actions, similar actions, and cumulative actions. Connected actions are those that are closely related (depend upon one another) and should be considered in the same EIS. Similar actions have similarities that merit their being considered together, even though they may not depend directly on one another. Cumulative actions are actions whose impacts are significant when considered together. The lead agency must consider reasonable alternatives to the proposed action, including no action, and must consider mitigation of environmental consequences. The range of alternatives discussed in an EIS shall encompass those to be considered by the decision maker. The lead agency must also identify and eliminate from detailed study issues that are not significant or that have been covered by prior environmental review. The lead agency must consider impacts that are direct, indirect, and/or cumulative. (Note that the word "cumulative" has been used in two ways: to refer to cumulative actions and to cumulative impacts.) Finally, the lead agency may hold scoping meetings to develop the scope of the EIS.

Some agencies require that an implementation plan be prepared to record the results of scoping and to guide preparation of the EIS. But this may become an end in itself, and the product may well be an elaborate document that requires much time and money to prepare and is of little use. For example, all of the scoping comments might be listed and answered individually. This is not necessary. As noted above, all that the agency must do during scoping is to determine the range of actions, alternatives, and impacts to be considered in the EIS. This will have been done, for the most part, before the NOI is prepared and can easily be completed in a summary implementation plan consisting of a very few pages after the agency reviews the scoping comments.

Preparation of the Draft EIS

Preparation of the draft EIS includes consideration of all of the items discussed in Chapter 5. The key points of the draft EIS are the alternatives and the environmental impacts of the alternatives. The rigor in an EIS lies in the accurate determination of the environmental impacts.

Preferred Alternative
(40 CFR 1502.14)

A preferred alternative should be identified in the draft EIS and must be identified in the final EIS if not identified in the draft EIS.

Agency Consultation
(40 CFR 1502.25)

Interagency consultation is strongly recommended with respect to any analyses required under the Fish and Wildlife Coordination Act, the National Historic Preservation Act, and the Endangered Species Act. This means that the lead agency should solicit a letter from the U.S. Fish and Wildlife Service and/or the National Marine Fisheries Service regarding any threatened or endangered species that may be present in the area of the proposed action or alternatives. The lead agency should also solicit a letter from the state historic preservation officer (SHPO) regarding any cultural or historic sites that may be present in the area of the proposed action or alternatives. Agencies should be prepared to conduct their own studies of threatened or endangered species and of cultural and historic sites. Impacts of the proposed action and alternatives on these species and sites should be discussed in the EIS. Mitigation of impacts should also be discussed in the EIS and must, in any event, be carried out under the Endangered Species Act, National Historic Preservation Act, and related acts. Also, if there are floodplains or wetlands at the site of the proposed action or alternatives, analyses of these conditions must be carried out and this can conveniently be done in the EIS. See Executive Orders 11988 and 11990 entitled "Floodplain Management" and "Protection of Wetlands," respectively.

Agency and EPA Notices of Availability, Draft EIS Distribution (40 CFR 1502.19, 1503.1, 1506.6, 1505.9, 1506.9, and 1506.10)

At a minimum, a notice of availability (NOA) of the draft EIS should be published in the *Federal Register* by the lead agency. The NOA should give a brief summary of the draft EIS; state how a copy may be obtained; give the name, address, and telephone number of a contact person; state the length of the comment period; and give the times, dates, and places of any public hearings on the draft EIS. The draft EIS must be filed with the EPA and should be distributed to agencies, organizations, and persons known to be interested in the EIS and to persons and agencies specifically requesting a copy. The EPA also publishes an NOA in the *Federal Register* that states that the EPA has received copies of the EIS. The EPA notice is separate from the agency notice and has implications with respect to the timing of further agency actions following publication of the draft or final EIS (40 CFR 1506.10).

Public Participation and Public Hearings (40 CFR 1502.5(c), 1503, and 1506.6)

The CEQ regulations strongly encourage both agency and public participation in the NEPA process and agency and public comment on the draft EIS.

If public hearings are held, they should be held in places of easy access to those who might be expected to be interested, i.e., in appropriate towns and cities, in locations with good parking and public transportation facilities, and at convenient times of day. The hearings should be conducted as information gathering hearings rather than as courtroom style hearings. That is, anyone should be allowed five minutes or so to speak (and, of course, should be allowed to submit written material of any length). Cross examination should not be permitted, with only clarifying questions from the hearing officer allowed. Ideally, the hearing officer should be the senior agency official in charge of preparation of the EIS. (Comments are directed to the authors of the EIS and the comments will have to be answered in the final EIS by the authors, so one of the authors should preside.) Often this is not done and some "impartial" hearing officer is selected, which wastes both time and money, but gives the agency a good feeling about its impartiality.

The agency should maintain a good mailing list that contains the names and addresses of agencies, groups, and individuals likely or known to be interested in the substance of the EIS.

Security should never be an issue at a public hearing on an EIS. Any demonstrators with signs should be invited into the hearing room, asked to place their signs around the outside of the room where they are visible, and invited to present comments on the EIS. Recessing the hearing will usually calm any boisterous behavior. Unpleasantness is possible, however, in those hearings where there is contention with individual property owners over eminent domain issues and the taking of private property.

It is not uncommon to precede public hearings with public meetings or workshops for the purposes of explaining the EIS to interested members and answering questions about the EIS. These workshops obviously must be staffed by the authors of the draft EIS. Appropriate displays and handouts should be provided.

Hearings may also be held early in the process of preparing the draft EIS for the purpose of gathering information for use in an EIS.

Materials related to the preparation of the EIS, as well as copies of the draft EIS and final EIS, should be placed in libraries or repositories with easy public access.

See Chapter 28 for a more complete discussion of public hearings.

Public and Agency Comments
(40 CFR 1500.4(l), 1503, and 1506.6)

The CEQ regulations strongly encourage public and agency comment on the draft EIS and provide for a 45-day comment period. The 45-day period is usually inadequate for those not on the initial distribution list, and comment periods up to 120 days are not uncommon. Agencies are expected to require comments to be as specific as possible in order to reduce paperwork. Cooperating agencies may comment on the draft EIS.

The Role of EPA, EPA Comments and Rating
(40 CFR 1504.1, 1506.9, and 1506.10)

The CEQ writes NEPA regulations. What then is EPA's role? Section 309 of the CAA directs EPA to review and comment on "any major Federal agency action . . . to which section 102(2)(C) of . . . [NEPA] applies." Section 309 also directs EPA to publish any determination that a federal action is "unsatisfactory from the standpoint of public health or welfare or environmental quality" and to refer the matter to the CEQ. EPA comments on and rates every draft and final EIS. EPA also publishes notices in the FR that draft and final EISs have been received by EPA. This may have important ramifications with respect to timing of subsequent agency action.

Pursuant to Section 309 of the CAA and Section 102(2)(c) of NEPA, the EPA reviews, provides comments on, and rates all draft and final EISs. The ratings are in two parts, a letter designation and a numerical designation, as follows:

LO—lack of objection	1—adequate
EC—environmental concerns	2—insufficient information
EO—environmental objections	3—inadequate
EU—environmentally unsatisfactory	

Ratings of EU and 3 are to be avoided. Ratings of EC, EO, and 2 on a draft EIS will usually be accompanied by comments from EPA, which if appropriately answered in the final EIS will result in a better rating of the final EIS by EPA.

Preparation of the Final EIS, Responses to Public and Agency Comments (40 CFR 1502.9, 1506.9, 1506.10, and 1508.4)

The lead agency is required to respond to substantive comments on the draft EIS. This response most frequently takes the form of stating the comment verbatim or paraphrasing and grouping several similar comments into a single comment. The agency's response is then printed following the comment in the final EIS. Any substantive change in the alternatives or in the analyses must appear in the final EIS. If there are no changes in the alternatives or analyses, then the draft EIS does not have to be rewritten. Rather, an addendum may be prepared that includes the comments and their responses, and any errata. Frequently, the letters and hearing comments are reprinted verbatim in the final EIS. The final EIS should be published in the same manner as the draft EIS and must be filed with the EPA. Copies should be sent to persons, agencies, and organizations on the mailing list for the draft EIS, as well as to persons commenting on the draft EIS.

The Record of Decision (40 CFR 1505.2 and 1506.10)

The EIS is an information disclosure document. It contains information on the alternatives and on the environmental impacts of the proposed action and alternatives. The ROD is a document that takes information from the EIS into account, but may include factors not in the EIS in the decision-making process. These other factors may include economic and technical considerations, as well as the agency's statutory missions. Thus, the environmentally preferred alternative need not be the alternative selected in the ROD. The ROD may not be published by the agency until 30 days after publication by the EPA of a notice in the *Federal Register* that the final EIS was filed with the EPA.

A question that frequently arises is whether or not commitments made in the ROD with respect to mitigation are legally enforceable.[2] Regrettably, they do not seem to be, even though the regulations indicate that they should be (40 CFR 1505.2).

REFERENCES

(1) "Environmental Quality, 25th Anniversary Report," Council on Environmental Quality, 1994-95.

(2) Dinah Bear, "NEPA at 19: A Primer on an 'Old' Law with Solutions to New Problems," *Environmental Law Reporter,* 19 ELR 10060-10069, February 1989.

Chapter 5	The Federal Environmental Impact Statement

The philosophy and format of an EIS are rather fully specified in the CEQ regulations, and the preparer of an EIS is well advised not to deviate from these instructions. This is because most of the legal action under NEPA is based on philosophy and format, and not on matters of substance. For example, lawsuits have been filed to force the agency to prepare an EIS when the agency has only prepared an EA, or when the plaintiff believes that the alternatives considered by the agency were inadequate. These lawsuits are filed in order to delay or stop the proposed action, and plaintiffs have found it easier to win on matters of form rather than substance.

General Instructions
(40 CFR 1502.1)

General instructions for preparing an EIS appear in several places in the CEQ regulations. "Environmental impact statements shall be concise, clear, and to the point . . ." (40 CFR 1500.2(b)). "Environmental impact statements shall be analytic rather than encyclopedic . . . . Impacts shall be discussed in proportion to their significance . . . . Environmental impact statements shall be kept concise and shall be no longer than absolutely necessary to comply with NEPA and with [the CEQ] regulations" (40 CFR 1502.2). "NEPA documents must concentrate on the issues that are truly significant to the action in question, rather than amassing needless detail . . . . NEPA's purpose is not to generate paperwork—even excellent paperwork—but to foster excellent action." (40 CFR 1500.1).

Unfortunately, the instructions to keep the EIS concise and to the point are often ignored. This is because an agency will prefer to include everything in order that the EIS will not be found later to be "inadequate" by some critic because something has been left out. The most important critics, are, of course, the EPA and the federal courts.

The EIS must treat all reasonable alternatives (including the proposed action) in substantial detail (40 CFR 1502.14), and should treat all alternatives, to the extent possible, with the same level of detail. Reasonable alternatives include those that are reasonably available to the federal government, not just those available to the lead agency. In addition, the EIS must be written in plain language (40 CFR 1502.8).

Content of the Draft EIS
(40 CFR 1502.10-1502.18)

"The following standard format for environmental impact statements should be followed unless the agency determines that there is a compelling reason to do otherwise: [The preparer of an EIS is advised not to do otherwise, because the agency's own internal reviewers may not able to understand doing otherwise.]

(a)   Cover sheet.
(b)   Summary.
(c)   Table of contents.

(d) Purpose of and need for action.

(e) Alternatives including proposed action.

(f) Affected environment.

(g) Environmental consequences.

(h) List of preparers.

(i) List of agencies, organizations, and persons to whom copies of the statement are sent.

(j) Index.

(k) Appendices (if any)."

Three additions to this list have appeared in recent EISs:

(l) Foreword.

(m) Introduction (which could include the statement on purpose and need).

(n) Applicable laws, regulations, and permits.

The subject and complexity of the EIS may require the addition of other sections (and multiple appendices), but these are special cases. Also, the alternatives section is sometimes simply called "Alternatives."

Cover Sheet
(40 CFR 1502.11)

The cover sheet should not exceed one page and should contain information listed in 40 CFR 1502.11.

Foreword

A foreword might be included if it is necessary to present information that cannot be conveniently accommodated elsewhere in the EIS. The foreword might include the following: information of a background nature that is required for an understanding of the overall context within which the EIS is placed, information of a procedural nature above and beyond that presented in the cover sheet, citation of the notice of intent to prepare the EIS, or a statement to the effect that the EIS has been prepared in compliance with the CEQ regulations. For the ordinary EIS, both a foreword and an introduction should not be necessary.

Summary
(40 CFR 1502.12)

The summary should adequately and accurately summarize the EIS, should state the agency's preferred alternative, and should stress the major conclusions, areas of controversy, and any issues to be resolved. The summary should ordinarily not exceed 15 pages.

It is sometimes convenient to number the sections of the summary in a manner equivalent to the numbers of the sections in the main body of the EIS. In that way, a direct cross reference is provided to readers from sections of the summary to sections of the body of the EIS.

Purpose and Need (40 CFR 1502.13); Introduction

The purpose and need statement must briefly state the proposed action, state the purpose of the proposed action, and specify the underlying need to which the agency is responding in proposing the alternatives including the proposed action.

Sometimes the purpose and need statement is a single statement and sometimes it is two separate statements, the two statements being the purpose of the proposed action and the need for the proposed action. Learned papers have been written on this point, but they are really irrelevant. Sometimes two statements are appropriate and at other times the purpose of the proposed action is also the need for the proposed action, and therefore a single statement will suffice.

If it is necessary to prepare an introduction, then the purpose and need statement should occupy a prominent subsection of its own in the introduction. An introduction may be necessary to include introductory material that is directly related to the EIS and that should be presented within the EIS proper, rather than outside the EIS in a foreword or cover sheet. (If that is the case, material in a numbered introduction can be included in a numbered summary; but it is awkward to include material from the cover sheet or foreword in the numbered summary if the cover sheet and foreword are not numbered sections of the EIS.) An important example of material that might be included in an introduction is a brief summary of the results of the scoping process, particularly if new actions, alternatives, or impacts are identified in the scoping process for inclusion in the EIS that were not identified in the notice of intent to prepare the EIS. Another example would be an explanation that the EIS has been written to accompany another regulatory process such as the CERCLA remedial investigation/feasibility study (RI/FS) process, if that were the case.

[Proposed Action and] Alternatives (40 CFR 1502.14)

The alternatives section should describe the proposed action and the alternatives, and should present the environmental impacts of the proposal and the alternatives in comparative form, based on the analyses presented in the environmental consequences section. The alternatives should be treated in substantial detail and with the same level of detail. The alternatives should be evaluated rigorously in order to define the issues sharply and to provide a clear basis for choice among the options. The alternatives must include the alternative of "no action." In NRDC v. Morton, the DC Circuit Court in 1972 held that an EIS must discuss all reasonable alternatives within the jurisdiction of any part of the federal government and that the EIS must discuss the environmental consequences of all of the reasonable alternatives.

Sometimes the proposed action can be generic rather than specific, and thus not one of the alternatives considered in detail. For example, in the Department of Energy's EIS on decommissioning the eight surplus plutonium production reactors at the Hanford Site, the proposed action was to decommission the eight reactors.[1] The alternatives considered in detail in the EIS were then no action, in-situ decommissioning, immediate one-piece removal, safe storage followed by one-piece removal, and safe storage followed by deferred dismantlement.

The alternatives section must include a brief discussion of the alternatives that were eliminated from detailed study and the reasons for their having been eliminated. The preferred alternative should be identified in the alternatives section in the draft EIS, if one exists. The preferred alternative must be identified in the final EIS, if not already identified in the draft EIS. The alternatives section should include "appropriate mitigation measures not already included in the proposed action or alternatives."

Affected Environment
(40 CFR 1502.15)

The affected environment section must succinctly describe the environment of the area(s) to be affected or created by the proposed action or the alternatives. The descriptions should be no longer than necessary to understand the effects of the alternatives and should be commensurate with the importance of the impacts. Verbose descriptions are not required.

The affected environment section should contain descriptions of the existing air quality, water quality, ecology, geohydrologic environment, radiological environment, noise environment, aesthetic environment, important transportation corridors, socio-economic environment, and historic significance of the area or any structures, as appropriate to the proposed action, and as adequate for an understanding of the impacts of the proposed action and the alternatives.

Environmental Consequences
(40 CFR 1502.16)

The environmental consequences section must form the scientific and analytic basis for the comparisons of the alternatives presented in the alternatives section. The discussion must include the environmental impacts of the proposed action and alternatives (i, iii), any adverse environmental effects which cannot be avoided should the proposal be implemented (ii), the relationship between short-term uses of man's environment and the maintenance and enhancement of long-term productivity (iv), and any irreversible or irretrievable commitments of resources that would be involved in the proposal should it be implemented (v). Stand-alone subsections for the latter three items (to show that they have not been neglected) are not uncommon. The Roman numerals in this paragraph are direct citations from NEPA (see Chapter 1).

A discussion in an EIS of irreversible or irretrievable commitments of resources has now become particularly important. This is because failure to include such a discussion can result in legal liabilities for the agency under other laws. For example Section 107(f)(1) of CERCLA provides that monetary damages may be assessed against agencies for injuries caused to natural resources from releases of hazardous substances, unless such injuries were specifically identified as irreversible and irretrievable commitments of natural resources in an environmental impact statement and unless the facility or project is operating within the terms of its permit.

Included in the environmental consequences section must be discussions of the following (40 CFR 1502.16):
(1) direct effects and their significance (40 CFR 1508.8);
(2) indirect effects and their significance (later in time or further in distance than direct impacts) (40 CFR 1508.8);
(3) possible conflicts between the proposed action (and/or alternatives) and the objectives of federal, regional, state, local, and/or Indian tribe land use plans, policies, and controls for the area concerned (40 CFR 1506.2(d));
(4) energy requirements and conservation potential of the alternatives, and mitigation measures;
(5) natural or depletable resource requirements and conservation potential of the alternatives, and mitigation measures;
(6) urban quality, historic and cultural resources, and the design of the built environment, including the reuse and conservation potential of the alternatives, and mitigation measures; and
(7) means to mitigate adverse environmental effects if not fully covered elsewhere (40 CFR 1502.14(f) and 1508.20).

Also included in the environmental consequences section, along with direct and indirect effects, must be a discussion of cumulative impacts (40 CFR 1508.7). See Chapter 6.

Finally, the environmental consequences section must contain discussions, to the extent that the subjects are important, of impacts on air quality; impacts on water quality; impacts from solid and hazardous waste production, management, and disposal; ecological impacts including impacts on threatened or endangered species; transportation impacts; noise impacts; aesthetic impacts; health impacts; impacts on cultural resources and historic properties; socioeconomic impacts; accidents; environmental justice; and probably soon: global warming.[2]

Applicable Laws, Regulations, and Permits (40 CFR 1502.25)

The standard CEQ format (40 CFR 1502.10) does not include a section on statutory and regulatory requirements. However, other provisions in the CEQ regulations make it very convenient for authors to add this section. These provisions are noted below, along with other items that may conveniently be included in the section on statutory and regulatory requirements.

The draft EIS must list all federal permits, licenses, and other entitlements that must be obtained in order to implement the proposal (40 CFR 1502.25). A discussion of the permits expected to be required is usually more appropriate than just a list. Also, because state permits now apply to some federal environmental activities, applicable state permits should also be discussed. These state permits arise because of waivers of sovereign immunity that are now contained in most federal environmental laws (see Chapter 10).

Applicable federal and state requirements, other than permit requirements, should be discussed, particularly those that include a numerical standard (the Safe Drinking Water Act regulations, for example), or a specific requirement that must be met (the Resource Conservation and Recovery Act regulations, for example). If not discussed elsewhere, interagency coordination, environmental analyses, and related surveys and studies required under the following acts should be discussed in the section on applicable laws, regulations, and permits (40 CFR 1502.25): the Fish and Wildlife Coordination Act, the National Historic Preservation Act, and the Endangered Species Act. Also compliance with floodplain/wetland environmental review requirements should be discussed here, if not elsewhere (Executive Orders 11988 "Floodplain Management" and 11990 "Protection of Wetlands"). If these discussions are extensive, they may be relegated to the appendices and summarized in the section on statutory and regulatory requirements. Sometimes cross references from the affected environment chapter to the statutory and regulatory requirements chapter are also appropriate.

Other Sections of an EIS

The sections devoted to the table of contents, list of preparers, distribution list, and index are self explanatory. Depending on the scope and complexity of the EIS, other major sections might be included. For example, the DOE EIS on ground water protection at the Savannah River Plant[3] includes a major section on "Studies and Monitoring." Generally, however, sticking closely to the CEQ's suggested chapter headings is recommended.

Appendices

Appendices should contain supporting data that are necessary for a full understanding of the material in the body of the EIS. Examples include lengthy, detailed calculations; descriptions of computer programs used to develop information in the EIS; computer outputs; and raw data.

REFERENCES

(1) *Draft Environmental Impact Statement on Decommissioning of Eight Surplus Production Reactors at the Hanford Site, Richland, Washington*, U.S. Department of Energy, DOE/EIS-0119D, March 1989.

(2) Dinah Bear, "NEPA at 19: A Primer on an 'Old' Law with Solutions to New Problems," *Environmental Law Reporter*, 19 ELR 10060-10069, February 1989.

(3) *Final Environmental Impact Statement of Waste Activities for Groundwater Protection, Savannah River Plant, Aiken, South Carolina*, U.S. Department of Energy, DOE/EIS-0120, December 1987.

This chapter contains a discussion of the environmental impacts that must be analyzed in an EIS. These impacts may be global, regional, and/or local, although it is usually local impacts that are given the most attention. Nevertheless, global and regional impacts are becoming increasingly important, and some of these are discussed briefly at the beginning of this chapter.

It is important to recognize that in an EIS, the chapter on the affected environment is also essentially a discussion of the impacts of the no action alternative. No action is, of course, keeping things as they are; and the impacts of keeping things as they are should be clear from the content of the affected environment chapter.

Impacts must be analyzed in substantial and reasonably equal detail for all alternatives. It is of particular importance to analyze carefully the impacts that may influence the choice of the preferred alternative. In the following sections, various environmental impacts that may be included in an EIS are discussed. They need to be discussed in the EIS only to the extent of their importance in impacting the environment or to the extent of their importance in selecting a preferred alternative.

Global and Regional Environmental Concerns

The total environmental impact from a human activity can be thought of as the product of the population and the per capita (per-person) environmental impact. Thus *both* population and per capita environmental impact contribute to total environmental impact; and, taken together, they compound the impact. (See Figure 5 for an example that utilizes the use of energy rather than a specific environmental impact.) *Increasing* either the population or the per capita impact will increase the total impact, and *increasing both* will compound the increase of the impact. On a local scale, or even on a small regional scale, this may not be serious. On a global scale, however, this is a prescription for disaster. This is because, at some time or another, the increasing environmental impact of a human activity cannot be contained within one or another of the natural cycles that occur on earth. Eventually some kind of ecological misfortune or disaster will result. These global concerns are not usually discussed in an EIS. Nevertheless, each environmental impact that cannot be accommodated within a natural cycle will eventually lead to a cumulative global effect. Recognition of this fact has been slow: ". . . environmental degradation occurs largely because people have been unwilling to add the costs of internalizing or closing the materials cycle and the costs of repairing the inevitable damage accompanying industrial activity to the price of things taken from the environment."[1] At some time in the future, global environmental impacts may well need to be discussed in EISs (see NEPA Section 102(F)).

An example of a global impact is global warming. In global warming, burning fossil fuels and other releases of carbon dioxide have led to increasing concentrations of carbon dioxide in the atmosphere. Carbon dioxide is a "greenhouse" gas because it transmits visible and ultraviolet radiation, but absorbs infrared radiation; i.e., carbon dioxide in the atmosphere lets visible and ultraviolet radiation from the sun pass through to the earth's surface but does not allow all of the infrared radiation (heat) returning from the earth to pass through to outer space, thus trapping heat in the earth's atmosphere and

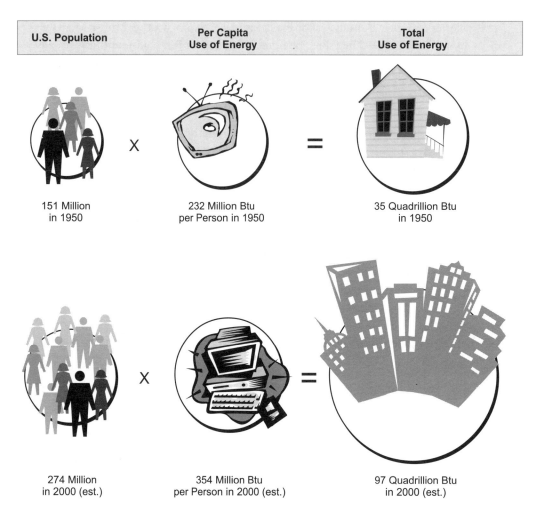

U.S. Population	Per Capita Use of Energy	Total Use of Energy

151 Million
in 1950

232 Million Btu
per Person in 1950

35 Quadrillion Btu
in 1950

274 Million
in 2000 (est.)

354 Million Btu
per Person in 2000 (est.)

97 Quadrillion Btu
in 2000 (est.)

Figure 5. Compound effect of population growth and per capita use of a resource. The example shown here is the use of energy in the United States between 1950 and 1990. The total use of energy in the U.S. has grown faster between 1950 and 1990 than either the population or the per capita use of energy alone. This compound effect has occurred with other energy and environmental resources.

giving rise to a gradual warming of the earth's surface. The earth will continue to warm until the concentration of carbon dioxide in the atmosphere reaches equilibrium and does not continue to increase, or until some other phenomenon causes a counteracting reduction in the earth's temperature. As long as the earth's population continues to increase and as long as our per-capita emission of carbon dioxide continues to increase, the concentration of carbon dioxide in the atmosphere will continue to increase and global warming will continue to increase. Other gases such as methane are also important greenhouse gases.

An example of both a global impact and a regional impact is the impact from the release of carbon dioxide, sulfur dioxide, and particulate matter from a coal-fired power plant. Carbon dioxide can contribute to atmospheric warming on a global basis. Sulfur dioxide can contribute to acid rain and decreased atmospheric visibility on a regional basis, and particulate matter can also contribute to decreased atmospheric visibility on a regional basis. Of course the latter two emissions (sulfur dioxide and particulate matter) can be mitigated by installing suitable control technologies. Carbon dioxide emissions, on the other hand, are not controlled.

Another regional impact of sorts is the impact from highways and high-voltage transmission lines. The impacts of the structures themselves are usually local from each local segment, but the extended linear nature of these facilities makes their impacts regional. If you don't believe this, just go to a few public hearings on a three-hundred-mile long high-voltage transmission line.

Analysis of Environmental Impacts

Air Emissions (Clean Air Act)

In an EIS, all emissions to the atmosphere must be identified and the impacts of these emissions on ambient air quality, on human health, and on the environment must be analyzed. The emissions to be analyzed can be found in 40 CFR 50—National Primary and Secondary Ambient Air Quality Standards, in 40 CFR 61—National Emission Standards for Hazardous Air Pollutants, and in 40 CFR 63— National Emission Standards for Hazardous Air Pollutants for Source Categories. Particulates, SO_2, CO, O_3, NO_2, and lead are the six "criteria pollutants" listed in the National Ambient Air Quality Standards. Hazardous air pollutants in 40 CFR 61 include Rn-222, Be, Hg, vinyl chloride, radionuclide emissions from DOE facilities, benzene, asbestos, and As. Hazardous air pollutants in 40 CFR 63 are the 189 listed by Congress in the Clean Air Act Amendments of 1990. Analyses may also need to be carried out for CO_2 and methane emissions (global warming or greenhouse effect) and for chlorofluorocarbon emissions (ozone layer depletion).

If emissions to the atmosphere are important for any alternative in the EIS, then a pathway analysis should be carried out for each emission. In a pathway analysis, the kind and amount of each emission must be known. These may be small routine emissions of various pollutants over extended periods of time or a large one-time emission of one or more pollutants from an accident. Each pollutant is traced from its source to various receptors (people, animals, crops, bodies of water, etc.); and the impact is determined based on the amounts released, on the speed and direction of winds, on the distribution of receptors, on the amounts or doses received by the receptors, and on dose-response data. Computer programs are available to assist in the calculations, but much data must be obtained by the EIS authors on the releases, wind patterns, receptor locations, and dose-response relationships in order to develop a credible prediction of the impacts.

Water Effluents (Clean Water Act, Safe Drinking Water Act)

In an EIS, effluents to bodies of water must be identified and the impacts of these effluents on ambient water quality (both surface and ground water), on drinking water quality (maximum contaminant levels and maximum contaminant level goals), on human health, and on the environment must be analyzed. Important water quality regulations (CWA) to be consulted include

- 40 CFR 122—The National Pollutant Discharge Elimination System (NPDES permit regulations)
- 40 CFR 122.2, which includes the following definition of pollutants: dredged spoil; solid waste, incinerator residue, filter backwash; sewage; garbage; sewage sludge; munitions; chemical wastes; biological materials; radioactive materials (except those regulated under the Atomic Energy Act); heat; wrecked or discarded equipment; rock; sand; cellar dirt; and industrial, municipal, and agricultural waste discharged into water
- 40 CFR 116—Designation of Hazardous Substances, which includes a list of 300 or so substances that are hazardous under the CWA which may or may not be covered by an NPDES permit
- 40 CFR 129—Toxic Pollutant Effluent Standards, which contains a short list of toxic organic pollutants
- And the SDWA regulations in 40 CFR 141—National Primary Drinking Water Regulations.

The list of regulated drinking water contaminants (SDWA) is getting longer rather rapidly. This list includes maximum contaminant levels (MCLs), which are legally enforceable with respect to drinking water, and maximum contaminant level goals (MCLGs), which are legally enforceable for cleanup actions under CERCLA. Pollutants also include suspended solids, biological oxygen demand (a measure of the amount of organic material present), pH (a measure of acidity), and fecal coliform bacteria (these are the so-called conventional pollutants), as well as the pollutants listed above, particularly hazardous pollutants such as heavy metals, radionuclides, and chlorinated organic compounds. The discharge of heat to any body of water may require a separate and lengthy analysis.

As in the case of air emissions, the impacts of water effluents may be analyzed by means of pathway analyses based on the kinds and amounts of pollutants discharged, on dilution in the receiving body of water, on amounts or doses received by people, animals, crops, etc., and on dose-response relationships. The calculations are, of course, different for pollutants released to surface water and for pollutants released to ground water. Computer programs are available to assist in the calculations; but again, as in the case of air emissions, complete and accurate input data are needed to develop a credible prediction.

Water Appropriation

The impacts of the appropriation of water from surface water sources and from ground water sources are becoming contentious issues now in many parts of the country, particularly in drought areas, in areas where rivers and streams are already over appropriated, and in areas where the life-cycles of anadromous fish are affected. The latter situations are doubly impacted by any endangered species declarations. Thus the impacts of any proposed water appropriation, for example for irrigation purposes or for cooling electric power plants, must be examined thoroughly in an EIS.

Solid Wastes (RCRA, CERCLA)

In an EIS, solid, hazardous, and radioactive wastes must be identified and their impacts analyzed on human health and the environment. Hazardous wastes (actually solid, liquid, and some gaseous wastes) are covered by RCRA and hazardous substances are covered by CERCLA. Wastes, i.e., CERCLA hazardous substances, already on the site from past treatment, storage, or disposal practices are covered by CERCLA, while new wastes created by the project are covered by RCRA. RCRA includes listed and characteristic wastes. The list appears in 40 CFR 261—Identification and Listing of Hazardous Waste. Characteristic wastes are those showing the characteristics of ignitability, corrosivity, reactivity, or toxicity (40 CFR 261.24). Other regulations to be consulted include 40 CFR 264, Appendix IX—Ground-Water Monitoring List. RCRA wastes do not include source, special nuclear, or by-product material (40 CFR 261.4(a)(4)), i.e., radioactive substances regulated under the Atomic Energy Act. Nevertheless, the impacts of radioactive wastes must be analyzed. CERCLA hazardous substances are those listed in 40 CFR 302 and include radioactive materials. All CERCLA hazardous substances need to be identified in the EIS because of the potential for accidental releases (regulated under CERCLA), and because of the potential for injury to natural resources and subsequent natural resource damage assessments (also covered under CERCLA). CERCLA hazardous substances may already exist in retired or abandoned waste disposal facilities on the proposed site; and therefore, if known to be present, must be identified in the EIS for impact analysis and for appropriate remedial action.

As in the cases of releases to the atmosphere or to bodies of water, pathway analyses must be carried out for the potential release of any hazardous substance or hazardous waste from waste facilities on the proposed site. These facilities may include treatment, storage, and/or disposal facilities. Computer programs are available to assist the EIS preparer; but again, substantial information must be gathered to provide input data to the computer programs. In the case of a waste burial ground, information about the following must be obtained: constituents of the waste, solubility of the waste constituents, dissolution rates of the waste constituents, rate of downward movement of the dissolved waste through the vadose zone, potential for adsorption of the dissolved wastes on soil particles, location of ground water, movement of the dissolved waste in the ground water, location of discharge points (wells or rivers), location and numbers of receptors, doses received by the receptors, and dose-response relationships. Again, computer programs are available to assist the EIS preparer.

Radionuclides

The potential release of radionuclides from a proposed facility or from a radioactive waste burial ground must be analyzed. Again, a pathway analysis is carried out that traces each radionuclide from its release point (stack, water effluent pipe, or burial ground) to the various receptors. The receptors, of course, can be human, plant, or other animal receptors. Impacts of releases of radionuclides to the atmosphere can be local (I-131), regional (I-131), or global (C-14). Because of public interest, very careful attention must be paid to the credibility of any calculations involving radionuclides.

Cultural and Historic Resource Preservation (National Historic Preservation Act) (40 CFR 1502.25)

A cultural resources survey of the area to be impacted by the project, consultation with the state historic preservation officer, and consultation with any Indian tribes that might be affected should be carried out as part of the EIS process to meet the historic preservation requirements of the National Historic Preservation Act (NHPA) during planning, construction, operation, and decommissioning, and also to meet the consultation requirements of 40 CFR 1502.25. Attention to the Archaeological Resources Protection Act, the Archaeological and Historic Preservation Act, the American Antiquities Act, the American Indian Religious Freedom Act, the Native American Graves Protection and Repatriation Act, and the Wild and Scenic Rivers Act is also appropriate. Any impacts on protected sites must be mitigated. Discovery of a protected structure, artifact, relic, or Indian burial ground can halt construction of a project and, in some instances, may result in relocation of the project.

As an example, the DOE in 1992 completed an EA on the construction and operation of the Environmental and Molecular Sciences Laboratory on the Columbia River at the Hanford Site.[2] The cultural resources survey conducted by the DOE's Pacific Northwest National Laboratory clearly indicated the possibility of the presence of Indian burials on the site. Indeed, Indian burials were discovered on the second day of construction. The laboratory was relocated further inland after the preparation of a new EA, the conduct of further cultural resource surveys,[3] and the consequent delay. Moral: pay attention to cultural and historic resources.

Land Use

Land use may be an important and even inflammatory local issue. Taking good farm land for any other purpose (power plants, industrial use, highways, roads, transmission lines, etc.), removing productive land behind dams, removing recreational land, and siting radioactive waste disposal facilities or hazardous waste management facilities can become land-use issues. "Prime farmland" is defined in the Department of Agriculture regulations in 7 CFR 657. Land use issues relating to linear features such as a road or high-voltage transmission line can be particularly troublesome because so many land owners are involved. Cultural resource issues, endangered species issues, and private property rights can become substantial land-use issues in the promotion of a project and in the accompanying EIS.

Endangered Species (Endangered Species Act) (40 CFR 1502.25)

Consultation with the U.S. Fish and Wildlife Service and/or the National Marine Fisheries Service, and the completion of a biological assessment, if required by the Endangered Species Act (ESA), should be carried out as part of the EIS process to meet the requirements of the Endangered Species Act and the consultation requirements of 40 CFR 1502.25. Endangered or threatened species and the critical habitat of such species are specifically protected. Attention to the Bald and Golden Eagle Protection Act and the Migratory Bird Treaty Act may also be appropriate as part of the EIS process. Even if a biological assessment is not required, a biological survey should be carried out; and any impacts on threatened or endangered species must be mitigated. Discovery onsite or even nearby of an endangered species can halt construction of a project.

Fish and Wildlife Coordination Act
(40 CFR 1502.25)

Almost any alteration of a body of water by a federal agency or licensed by a federal agency requires consultation with the U.S. Fish and Wildlife Service and with the state wildlife authority to conserve wildlife resources. This should be done as part of the EIS process. Full discussion of the impacts should be presented in the EIS.

Floodplain/Wetland Analysis
(40 CFR 1502.25)

Executive Orders 11988 and 11990 require federal agencies to carry out flood-plain and wetland analyses. Inclusion in the EIS is appropriate. Any wetland loss should be explained, particularly if a Corps of Engineers permit for the discharge of dredged or fill material is required. Mitigation of wetland loss should be discussed. Important to the discussion of wetlands is the definition of a wetland. Different agencies have different definitions for what constitutes a wetland. The DOE definition of wetland in 10 CFR 1022.4(v) is: " 'Wetlands' means those areas that are inundated by surface or groundwater with a frequency sufficient to support and under normal circumstances does or would support a prevalence of vegetative or aquatic life that requires saturated or seasonally saturated soil conditions for growth and reproduction. Wetlands generally include swamps, marshes, bogs, and similar areas such as sloughs, potholes, wet meadows, river overflow, mudflats, and natural ponds." Impacts from floods, particularly 100- and 500-year floods, must be examined (10 CFR 1022 for DOE). The Federal Emergency Management Agency (FEMA) has prepared floodplain maps for many parts of the U.S., but not usually for federally owned lands.

Ecological Impacts

Ecological impacts not already considered (such as habitat destruction or alteration, noise pollution, impact on species in general, and impact on any particularly sensitive species or ecosystem) must be included in the EIS. Many examples can be cited, such as any impact on salmon in the Columbia River system because of listing certain salmon runs in the Snake River as threatened or endangered species; any impact on old-growth forests in the Pacific Northwest because of listing the spotted owl; any modification or removal of wetlands in a major migratory bird flyway; destruction of forests in a river tributary system; impacts of thermal discharges on bodies of water and their flora and fauna; and impacts on wild, scenic, or recreational rivers.

Accidents

The impacts of accidents during construction, operation, and decommissioning must be included in an EIS. Accidents include industrial accidents, transportation accidents, and accidental releases of hazardous substances (see Chapter 9). Impacts include those on the environment, as well as those on human health. Pathway analyses of accidental releases of hazardous substances should be carried out. As pointed out below, the EIS need not speculate on the worst imaginable accident. Only credible, though highly improbable, accidents need be discussed.

Health Effects

Health effects of the proposed action and alternatives must be evaluated and discussed in the EIS. Good statistics are available from which to estimate the number and kinds of industrial and transportation accidents (see Chapter 9). Health effects, however, from routine or accidental releases of hazardous substances are much more difficult to estimate. Computer programs exist, but a substantial amount of input data is required to make the calculations.

Unusual Impacts or Impacts not Covered by Major Environmental Laws

Most environmental impacts that must be discussed in an EIS are also dealt with in major environmental laws such as the CAA, CWA, SDWA, RCRA, CERCLA, ESA, NHPA, and so on. Other impacts are obvious such as transportation impacts, socioeconomic impacts, and general ecological impacts. But outside of these "standard" impacts are other impacts from facilities such as high-voltage transmission lines. In the case of high-voltage transmission lines, these impacts include electric and magnetic field effects on humans and other species, corona discharge effects on radio and television transmission, and any effects of induced spark discharges from nearby large metal objects. Impacts such as these must be discussed in an EIS when appropriate.

Socioeconomic Impacts
(40 CFR 1508.14)

Socioeconomic effects are not intended by themselves to require an EIS. But when an EIS is prepared and economic or social and natural or physical environmental effects are interrelated, then the EIS must discuss all of those effects on the human environment. Socioeconomic impacts include the impacts of construction, operation, and decommissioning on the local and regional infrastructure, including schools, housing, police protection, fire protection, medical services, hospitals, roads, traffic, recreation, etc. Socioeconomic impacts can be both direct and indirect. Obviously, a substantial amount of data must be gathered.

Environmental Justice

Executive Order 12898 of February 11, 1994, entitled "Federal Actions to Address Environmental Justice in Minority Populations and Low-Income Populations," requires each agency of the federal government to make "environmental justice part of its mission by identifying and addressing, as appropriate, disproportionately high and adverse human health or environmental effects of its programs, policies, and activities on minority populations and low-income populations . . ." This means that minority and low-income populations need to be identified in an EIS when these populations are in close proximity to the proposed action or alternatives, and any disproportionate effects identified and mitigated.

Population Growth

Projected population growth over the lifetime of the project should be discussed in an EIS as part of socioeconomic impacts.

Depletion of Resources
(40 CFR 1502.16(f))

Use of and depletion of nonrenewable resources such as fuels, ores, and soils (i.e., soil erosion) should be discussed for the life cycle of the project.

Energy Requirements
(40 CFR 1502.16(e))

If not discussed in the section on depletion of nonrenewable resources, energy requirements should be discussed in a separate section. The discussion should include a life-cycle discussion of all fuels to be used in the project, beginning with vehicle fuels used during construction. Fuels used during operation should be discussed including oil, gas, coal, nuclear, solar power, wind power, and hydro power. Energy used during decommissioning or closure should also be discussed.

Transportation Impacts

For many proposed actions, transportation of goods, materials, and/or wastes is an important part of the proposed action or alternatives. Transportation should be analyzed in terms of energy use, transportation routes, volume of traffic, routine traffic accidents, and accidents involving releases of hazardous or radioactive substances. Often a programmatic EIS involving different sites throughout the country will require a very extensive transportation analysis.

Irreversible or Irretrievable Commitments of Resources
(40 CFR 1502.16)

In any EIS prepared by a federal agency, special consideration is now required if there is any possibility of an irreversible or irretrievable commitment of resources. This is because of the natural resource damage assessment provision in CERCLA (42 USC 9607(f)), which states that "In the case of an injury to, destruction of, or loss of natural resources . . . liability shall be to the United States Government and to any State for natural resources within the State or belonging to, managed by, controlled by, or appertaining to such State and to any Indian tribe for natural resources belonging to, managed by, controlled by, or appertaining to such tribe . . . Provided, however, that no liability to the United States or State or Indian tribe shall be imposed . . . where the party sought to be charged has demonstrated that the damages to natural resources complained of were specifically identified as an irreversible and irretrievable commitment of natural resources in an environmental impact statement, or other comparable environment analysis, and the decision to grant a permit or license authorizes such commitment of natural resources, and the facility was otherwise operating within the terms of its permit or license . . ."

This is perhaps the only place where an EIS takes on a substantive role rather than merely a procedural role. Clearly, this is an item that must not be overlooked in preparing an EIS.

Direct and Indirect Impacts
(40 CFR 1502.16(a) and 1508.8)

Direct and indirect impacts need to be discussed for all of the impacts listed above. Remember that direct impacts are those that are caused by the action and that occur at the time and place of the action. Indirect impacts are those that are also caused by the action, are reasonably foreseeable, and occur removed in time or distance from the action.

Mitigation

(40 CFR 1502.16(h) and 1508.20)

Mitigation of adverse impacts must be discussed in an EIS. It must also be recognized that suggestions for mitigation may become promises in the ROD. Mitigation includes avoiding the impact, minimizing the impact, rectifying the impact, reducing or eliminating the impact, and/or compensating for the impact (1508.20).

Worst Case Analysis
(40 CFR 1502.22)

The CEQ recently changed its regulations regarding incomplete or unavailable information. The amended regulations require that the agency disclose that the information is lacking and that the agency apply a "rule of reason" approach to the evaluation of impacts that depend on the unavailable information. The information must be obtained, however, if the cost is not too great. The amended rule replaces a rule that required a "worst case analysis" of the impacts that depend on the missing information. Recent court cases, however, have clouded the issue by requiring that worst case analyses be carried out without remanding the amended regulation to CEQ. In the past, the worst case analysis frequently involved the most serious accident imaginable.

Risk Analysis

The CEQ regulations do not explicitly require formal risk analyses, although some human impact analyses (or pathway analyses) may closely approximate risk analyses. Risk is a probability and a risk analysis is an analysis of the probability of something happening, usually a health effect, injury, or death. Frequently, risk analyses report the number of consequences of normal operation, or the number of consequences from an accident and the expected frequency of the accident, rather than the actual risk. See Chapter 9.

Cumulative Impacts
(40 CFR 1508.7)

A discussion of cumulative impacts must be presented in the EIS. Cumulative impacts include those from similar existing or reasonably foreseeable future activities in the vicinity of the proposed action and its alternatives.

Modeling of Impacts

Many computer programs are now available to assist the EIS writer in evaluating various impacts of construction, operation, and transportation. Many of these programs belong to the federal agencies that prepare EISs and thus are in the public domain and are available to others. Since these programs change frequently, the best way to learn about them is to read recent EISs and call the authors. See Chapter 1 for information on locating EISs.

REFERENCES

(1)   Robert V. Bartlett, *The Reserve Mining Controversy*, Indiana University Press, 1980.

(2)   *Environmental Assessment for the Environmental and Molecular Sciences Laboratory at the Hanford Site, Richland, Washington*, U.S. Department of Energy, DOE/EA-0429, September 1992.

(3)   *Environmental Assessment for the Resiting, Construction, and Operation of the Environmental and Molecular Sciences Laboratory at the Hanford Site, Richland, Washington*, U.S. Department of Energy, DOE/EA-0959, July 1994.

Chapter 7　Other NEPA-Related Matters

Agency Procedures
(40 CFR 1507)

The CEQ regulations direct federal agencies to comply with the CEQ regulations, to prepare EISs, and to adopt procedures to supplement the CEQ regulations. Procedures are to be promulgated in the CFR with due regard for the Administrative Procedure Act. Agencies usually adopt the CEQ regulations and promulgate their own supplemental regulations, for example the Department of Energy in 10 CFR 1021, the Department of Defense in 32 CFR 188, and the Nuclear Regulatory Commission in 10 CFR 51. Agencies may, in their procedures, identify actions that normally require EAs, actions that normally require EISs, and actions that do not require either an EA or an EIS (categorical exclusions). Agencies may prepare classified EISs. EPA gets special treatment: see "Functional Equivalence" in Chapter 4.

Limitations on Agency Actions
(40 CFR 1502.2(f) and 1506.1)

"Agencies shall not commit resources prejudicing selection of alternatives before making a final decision." "Until an agency issues a record of decision . . ., no action concerning the proposal shall be taken which would: (1) Have an adverse environmental impact; or (2) Limit the choice of reasonable alternatives." In 1992, the DOE purchased $10 million worth of components for a mixed waste incinerator at Savannah River before completing an EA and reaching a FONSI. This was a violation of NEPA and the CEQ regulations. But there is no penalty under NEPA for this kind of violation, except possibly delay of the project in order to complete an EA or EIS.

"Interim actions" may be carried out while an EIS is being prepared if the action is justified independently of the program, if a separate EIS is prepared, and if the interim action will not prejudice the decision on the larger EIS.

Again, in spite of proscriptions such as the ones above, there are no penalties for violating NEPA except for a delay to complete an EA or EIS or to prepare a supplemental EIS.

Judicial Review (Case Law)
(40 CFR 1500.3)

Judicial review of an agency action is, at the outset, based on procedural issues rather than substantive issues, i.e., courts are reluctant to substitute their technical judgement for an agency's technical judgement. In general, when reviewing an agency action, courts look for 1) did the agency act within its statutory authority; 2) was the action arbitrary, capricious, or an abuse of discretion; and 3) were appropriate procedures followed? In the case of NEPA, an agency satisfies NEPA by preparing an adequate EIS.[1] An inadequate EIS is merely returned to the agency and is repaired by the agency, not by the court. The CEQ's intention is that judicial review of an agency's compliance with the CEQ regulations not occur before the agency has filed a final EIS, has reached a FONSI, or takes action that will result in irreparable harm. Recently, about 100 lawsuits involving NEPA have been filed each year.[2] Most of these lawsuits claimed that an agency had prepared an inadequate EIS or that an agency had failed to prepare an EIS when one was required.

Adequacy of the EIS

Early court challenges under NEPA were more on the basis of failure to prepare an EIS (Calvert Cliffs decision) than on the basis of adequacy. Nevertheless, court challenges have been made, and won, on the basis that the EIS was "inadequate." And inadequacy usually means that not all of the CEQ requirements for the contents of the EIS were met. This also means that EISs are big because the agency cannot afford to leave anything out.

Conflict of Interest (40 CFR 1506.5(c))

The CEQ regulations provide for the preparation of an EIS by a contractor under agency guidance, provided that the contractor has no conflict of interest, i.e., has no financial interest in the outcome of the project. This precludes the preparation of an EIS by an operating contractor who will be in charge of building and/or operating the facility, but does not preclude the operating contractor from furnishing information for the EIS upon request. An EA may be prepared for a federal agency by any contractor.

Forty Questions

CEQ published additional guidance under the title, "Forty Most Asked Questions Concerning CEQ's National Environmental Policy Act Regulations" in the *Federal Register* on March 23, 1981 (46 FR 18026). Subsequent guidance appeared in 48 FR 34263, July 28, 1983, under the title, "Guidance Regarding NEPA Regulations."

Standing

"Standing" is the requirement that only persons with a direct stake in the outcome of a disagreement may use the courts to settle the disagreement. Standing to sue under NEPA or other environmental laws was once based on clear economic harm to specific individuals. But Sierra Club v. Morton in 1975 (not a NEPA case) changed this. Sierra Club lost this case for want of standing. However, the Supreme Court then went on to define standing, essentially to the benefit of environmentalists. For a long time, standing was available to environmental groups on the basis of the interest dealt with in the statute, i.e., injury did not have to be an economic harm to a specific individual, but could be on the basis of environmental interests.[1] This is now changing, although citizens are granted standing explicitly in CAA, CWA, and the Noise Control Act. In National Wildlife Federation v. Lujan (the Scalia decision), the Supreme Court in 1990 returned to the restriction in Article III of the U.S. Constitution that court cases deal with "cases" and "controversies" and therefore that standing requires actual "injury in fact" [to an individual].[3] The Supreme Court also made a similar decision in Lujan v. Defenders of Wildlife in 1992. See Spensely, "National Environmental Policy Act," in Sullivan, et al.[4] for a discussion of standing.

Expansion of Agency Authority under NEPA (to deny or condition an action), the Taking Issue

Can an agency's denial of a privately proposed action under NEPA be construed to be a "taking" entitled to compensation under the due process clause? Cases have reached the courts in which the denial of an environmental permit was construed to be a taking subject to compensation. In 1990, a U.S. Claims Court awarded Florida Rock Industries one million dollars because the U.S. Army Corps of Engineers denied Florida Rock Industries a permit to dredge and fill wetlands on its property (Florida Rock Industries v. U.S.). Cases of this kind under NEPA have not yet reached the courts, i.e., the denial of a private action because it was not selected by a federal agency in its record of decision. It is only a matter of time.

Federal Environmental Law

Most EISs now include a more expansive discussion of environmental law and other requirements than just the "federal permits, licenses, and other entitlements" required by 40 CFR 1502.25(b). These federal environmental laws and requirements include the CAA, CWA, SDWA, RCRA, CERCLA, species protection acts, historic preservation acts, floodplain/wetland reviews, and transportation requirements. Major federal permits discussed in EISs include the CAA air quality permit, which may include the old prevention of significant deterioration (PSD) permit and the National Emission Standards for Hazardous Air Pollutants (NESHAP) permit; the CWA National Pollutant Discharge Elimination (NPDES) permit; the RCRA treatment, storage, or disposal (TSD) permit; the RCRA underground storage tank (UST) permit; the SDWA underground injection control (UIC) permit; the Corps of Engineers (COE) Rivers and Harbors Act Section 10 permit for work in navigable waters; and/or the COE CWA Section 404 permit for discharge of dredged or fill material into waters of the United States.

Because environmental law largely dictates what must be considered in an EIS, the latter part of this book is devoted entirely to environmental law.

Emergencies (40 CFR 1506.11)

"Where emergency circumstances make it necessary to take an action with significant environmental impact without observing the provisions of these regulations, the Federal agency taking the action should consult with the Council about alternative arrangements."

Pre 1970 Actions (40 CFR 1506.12(b))

"NEPA shall continue to be applicable to actions begun before January 1, 1970 to the fullest extent possible." This statement in the regulations would seem to make NEPA applicable before it was passed. Few agencies have looked very far backward, but many have prepared new environmental documentation for expansions of activities that existed in 1970.

REFERENCES

(1)   S. K. Fairfax, "A Disaster in the Environmental Movement," *Science*, 199, 743, 17 February 1978.

(2)   "Environmental Quality, 25th Anniversary Report," Council on Environmental Quality, 1994-95.

(3)   K. Sheldon, "NWF v. Lujan: Justice Scalia Restricts Environmental Standing to Constrain the Courts," 20 ELR 10577, December 1990.

(4)   Thomas F. P. Sullivan, et al., *Environmental Law Handbook*, Fifteenth Edition, Government Institutes, 1999.

Chapter 8 — State Environmental Policy Acts

Many states have passed environmental policy acts that apply to state agencies. These state environmental policy acts and their regulations are usually very similar to NEPA and the CEQ regulations, but may differ in detail.

Applicability of State Environmental Policy Acts to Federal Activities

There is no waiver of sovereign immunity in NEPA, so state environmental policy acts do not apply to federal activities. However, NEPA, in Section 102(D), speaks to the preparation of federal EISs by state agencies (with federal approval), and the CEQ regulations speak to the elimination of duplication in the preparation of environmental documentation and provide for federal-state cooperation that includes joint federal-state EISs and joint federal-state lead agencies (40 CFR 1506.2).

Chapter 9 — Risk Assessment

When the impacts of constructing, operating, and/or decommissioning a proposed facility are discussed in an EIS, the consequences of these activities and the consequences of releases of hazardous substances must be included in the discussion. Frequently, the term "risk" is used in describing these consequences. Unfortunately, "risk" is not always well defined, is sometimes improperly defined, or, worse, is given more than one meaning in the same EIS. To add to the confusion, risk may be actual risk, calculated risk, or perceived risk.

Risk, in its narrowest quantitative meaning, is a probability; it is a number between zero and one; and it means the probability of loss, injury, sickness, or death. Risk is the number of consequences in a population divided by the population. Furthermore, risk applies to populations of persons and not to individuals; i.e., the risk to a given individual cannot be identified, but the risk to a number of individuals in a large population can, in theory, be determined. Documents, including those published by the EPA, frequently imply that risk can be determined for individuals. This is not the case. Risks are estimated for populations and therefore apply to populations.

Actual risks are those that may be determined directly from existing human statistical data. Good statistical data are available on different types of construction accidents and on automobile accidents. These data are available from the National Safety Council (NSC) (see Chapter 1). Good data are also available on the effects of radiation based on the work of the Committee on the Biological Effects of Radiation.[1] These data are, however, less definitive than the data on accidents.

Calculated risks are those for which good human statistical data are not available, but for which data are available from animal studies. The risks from releases of hazardous substances to the environment fall into this category. For these risks a three-step process is employed.[2]

- Hazard identification: determine the identities and qualities of the hazardous substances that are released.

- Exposure assessment: determine conditions under which people could be exposed and the doses that occur as the result of exposure.

- Dose-response assessment: determine the incidences of adverse effects from the doses.

The dose-response relationship must be calculated based on responses extrapolated from high animal doses to low animal doses, and on responses extrapolated from low animal doses to low human doses. The risk, then, becomes the number of effects divided by the total population under consideration. Dose-response information is tabulated by the EPA in its Integrated Risk Information System (IRIS). (See Chapter 1.)

Perceived risks are those in the mind of the beholder and may be accurate, incorrect, or nonexistent.

Obviously, only actual risks can be given much credence. Nevertheless, entire regulatory scaffolds have been constructed based on calculated risks and many EISs have reported environmental impacts based on calculated risks. Little can be done about improving calculated risks until better human data are available, and this is likely to be never because of the difficulty of obtaining human data.

Reporting the risk of some activity or event in an EIS as a single number is generally not a useful exercise. What should be reported is the number of consequences in a population and the total population under consideration. For example, in the case of industrial accidents, the total number of construction accidents can be determined and reported, based on the number of person-hours worked and known accident statistics from tables published by the NSC. The total number of construction workers should also be reported. Another example would be the risk from an accidental release of radioactivity. The expected frequency of that particular accident can be reported (number per year), the number of latent cancer fatalities in the surrounding population can be calculated (by a series of less than easy calculations) and reported, and the number of persons in the surrounding population can be reported. A third example would be the risk from routine releases of radionuclides over an extended period of time, say a year. Again, the number of latent cancer fatalities can be calculated in a population and reported along with the population involved. Of course it should be mentioned that the releases are occurring over a year. Numbers such as these are much more useful than a single "risk" number, although the risk can still be calculated by dividing the number of consequences by the population under consideration. Risk alone, however, does not necessarily carry with it the time period over which the risk occurs.

Careful consideration of risk in an EIS is required in order not to end up with a mess that demonstrates lack of credibility.

REFERENCES

(1)   *Health Effects of Exposure to Low Levels of Ionizing Radiation—BEIR V*, Committee on the Biological Effects of Ionizing Radiation of the National Research Council, National Academy Press, 1990.

(2)   *Risk Assessment and Risk Management in Regulatory Decision-Making*, Commission on Risk Assessment and Risk Management, 1997.

Chapter 10 — Federal Environmental Law

The last half of this book contains a discussion of federal environmental laws and regulations. The discussion is necessary because authors of EISs must be familiar with federal environmental laws in order not to neglect any important environmental issue in the EIS. State environmental laws are not discussed; but they may complement, duplicate, or even arise from federal law. Federal environmental laws apply to federal facilities; and, in those cases where Congress has provided a waiver of sovereign immunity, state environmental laws apply to federal facilities.

Environmental standards and permit requirements usually appear in regulations and not in the laws themselves. Thus, we place somewhat more emphasis on regulations and somewhat less on laws. Material has been taken primarily from the laws and regulations themselves as cited in the text. For a more complete discussion of environmental law, other than species protection and historic preservation laws, see T. F. P. Sullivan, et al.[1]

An introduction to environmental law has already been provided in Chapter 1 and will not be repeated here.

Waivers of Sovereign Immunity

Activities of the federal government are not ordinarily subject to regulation by the states. This federal supremacy or sovereign immunity (Article V, Section 2, of the U.S. Constitution) was affirmed by the Supreme Court in M'Culloch v. Maryland. The Supreme Court said, "The government of the Union, though limited in its powers, is supreme within its sphere of action." Sovereign immunity means that states cannot tell the federal government what to do without the federal government's permission or that one cannot sue the federal government without the federal government's permission. In environmental law, however, Congress has provided waivers of sovereign immunity so that states can regulate some environmental activities of the federal government and citizens can sue the federal government over certain environmental matters.

These waivers of sovereign immunity appear in Section 118 of the CAA, Section 313 of the CWA, Section 1447 of the SDWA, Section 6001 of RCRA, and Section 120 of CERCLA. The waivers of sovereign immunity provide either for the delegation of environmental regulatory authority over federal facilities to the states, usually by the U.S. EPA, or provide for the outright regulation of federal facilities by the states without delegation by the EPA. Case law has usually held that the waiver must be clear and unmistakable to be valid. The Federal Facilities Compliance Act (FFCA) was enacted by Congress in 1992 to make the waiver of sovereign immunity in RCRA more clear and less mistakable.

National Environmental Policy Act

NEPA applies to agencies of the federal government and requires agencies to prepare an environmental impact statement for any major federal action significantly affecting the quality of the human environment. NEPA and the NEPA regulations are discussed in the first nine chapters of this book and are not repeated here.

REFERENCE

(1)   Thomas F. P. Sullivan, et al., *Environmental Law Handbook*, Fifteenth Edition, Government Institutes, 1999.

The Clean Air Act (42 USC 7401 et seq.) was enacted, after predecessor laws, in 1970 and was amended in 1977 and in 1990. It deals both with stationary sources of air pollutants (factories, refineries, power plants, etc.) and with mobile sources of air pollutants (airplanes and automobiles). It provides for the establishment of "National Ambient Air Quality Standards" (NAAQS, Sec. 109); provides for the creation of "State Implementation Plans" (SIP, Sec. 110), which are to be approved by EPA to allow states to impose controls on stationary sources to reduce emissions to meet NAAQSs; provides for "New Source Performance Standards" (NSPS, Sec. 111), to be applied to new or modified industrial stationary sources; provides for the "Prevention of Significant Deterioration" (PSD, Sec. 160-190) of air quality from new or modified sources in regions that already meet the NAAQSs; and provides for the creation of "National Emission Standards for Hazardous Air Pollutants" (NESHAP, Sec. 112). Three major permits or authorizations were established in the CAA: PSD, NESHAP, and nonattainment area. These three permits are evolving into a single air quality permit under the Clean Air Act Amendments of 1990, which will include toxic sources (NESHAPs), attainment area sources (PSD), nonattainment area sources, and sources subject to NSPS. This single permit includes some facilities not subject to permit before 1990. Also, a waiver of sovereign immunity is included in the CAA (Sec. 118). Chlorofluorocarbons (protection of the ozone layer) and acid rain are also covered in the CAA.

The NAAQSs are not directly enforceable in and of themselves. Rather, they set the standards on which other enforceable requirements, such as emission limitations and permit requirements, are based. Permits were not required for existing sources before 1990, unlike existing sources under the Clean Water Act. Now CAA permits will apply to all major sources of criteria air pollutants, as well as to sources of hazardous air pollutants.

The 1990 amendments to the CAA keep the basic substance of the CAA intact and add a number of additional requirements. For example, the use of substances most destructive to the ozone layer must be phased out by the year 2000; pollution from automobiles is supposed to be reduced by 90 percent in 10 to 20 years, partly from reformulated gasolines emitting 25 percent less volatile organic compounds by the year 2000 in the worst ozone attainment areas; electric utility sulfur dioxide emissions that cause acid rain are to be reduced by 50 percent in 10 to 20 years; and toxic pollutant emissions (NESHAPs) from industry are to be reduced by 90 percent in 10 to 20 years. Also, air quality permits are both consolidated and broadened to cover essentially all major sources and all new plants. The CAA permits are now more comprehensive like the CWA permits.

Title I of the CAA Amendments of 1990, Attainment and Maintenance of NAAQS, establishes new requirements for ozone and carbon monoxide nonattainment areas. Title II, Mobile Sources, is directed at reducing pollution from mobile sources. Title III, Hazardous Air Pollutants, lists 189 hazardous air pollutants that EPA must regulate by the year 2000 (adds to NESHAPs). Title IV, Acid Deposition Control, places further restrictions on the emission of sulfur dioxide and oxides of nitrogen. Title V, Permits, revises the existing permit system to require EPA, state, or local permits for emitters of more than 100 tons per year of criteria pollutants under Title I, for electric utilities regulated under Title IV, and for sources that emit more than 10 tons per year of one hazardous air pollutant or 25 tons per year of a combination of pollutants under Title I. Title VI, Stratospheric Ozone Protection, mandates the elimination of substances most destructive to the ozone layer. "Maximum achievable control technology" (MACT) will be required.

EPA's Air Quality Regulations (40 CFR 50-99)

Federal regulations implementing the CAA appear in the Code of Federal Regulations, Title 40, Sections 50 through 99 (40 CFR 50-99). Significant EPA air quality regulations include the following:

40 CFR 50, "National Primary and Secondary Ambient Air Quality Standards" (CAA Sec. 109)

EPA regulations in 40 CFR 50 set ambient air quality standards for air pollutants including sulfur oxides, particulate matter, carbon monoxide, ozone, nitrogen dioxide, and lead (criteria pollutants). The primary standards are to protect the public health with an adequate margin of safety, and the secondary standards are to protect the public welfare (although the secondary standards are often the same as the primary standards). Protection of the public welfare (CAA Sec. 302(h)) means protection against harm to soils, water, crops, vegetation, man-made materials, animals, wildlife, weather, visibility, climate, property, transportation, economic values, and protection of personal comfort and well-being.

40 CFR 51-52, State Implementation Plans (CAA Sec. 110)

The regulations in 40 CFR 51-52 establish the requirements for state implementation plans and record the approved plans. The State Implementation Plans (SIPs) are directed at the control of emissions from stationary sources to meet NAAQSs. SIPs must require permits for the construction and operation of new or modified stationary sources anywhere in a nonattainment area, under Sec. 172 of the CAA. "Reasonably available control technology" (RACT) can be required. States can also regulate radionuclide emissions (CAA Sec. 116, 118, and 122), including radionuclide emissions from federal facilities.

40 CFR 60, "Standards of Performance for New Stationary Sources" (CAA Sec. 111)

EPA regulations in 40 CFR 60 provide standards for the control of the emission of pollutants to the atmosphere from a number of different sources listed in 40 CFR 60. Construction or modification of an emissions source may require a prevention of significant deterioration of air quality permit under 40 CFR 51.166 or 52.21 in areas that already meet the NAAQSs. A PSD permit may require the use of best available control technology (BACT). These regulations are also called "new source performance standards."

40 CFR 61, "National Emission Standards for Hazardous Air Pollutants," and 40 CFR 63, "National Emission Standards for Hazardous Air Pollutants for Source Categories" (NESHAP) (CAA Sec. 112)

EPA hazardous emission standards in 40 CFR 61 provide for the control of the emission of hazardous pollutants to the atmosphere, including radon-222 from underground uranium mines and from uranium mill tailings, beryllium, mercury, vinyl chloride, radionuclides from DOE facilities, benzene, asbestos, and arsenic. Approval to construct a new facility or to modify an existing one may be required by these regulations (NESHAP approval). Hazardous air pollutants are those that "may reasonably be anticipated to result in an increase in mortality, or an increase in serious irreversible, or incapacitating reversible illness" (CAA Sec. 112(a)(1)). [In environmental law, "hazardous" usually means impacting human health.] NESHAPs apply to existing, as well as new, sources. Pollutants regulated under NESHAPs are considered to be localized problems, not sufficiently broad to be placed under the NAAQSs. Substantial additions are being made by EPA to the list of hazardous air pollutants in 40 CFR 61, based on the 189 hazardous air pollutants listed by Congress in the Clean Air Act Amendments of 1990. These additions appear in 40 CFR 63.

40 CFR 70 and 71, EPA's Operating Permits Programs

The regulations in 40 CFR 70 cover state operating permit requirements for all of the presently regulated pollutants, as well as the new pollutants to be regulated under the Clean Air Act Amendments. The regulations in 40 CFR 71 cover EPA administration of the operating permits program in those states where the state program is not yet functioning.

Chapter 12   Clean Water Act

The Clean Water Act (33 USC 1251 et seq.) was enacted in 1972 as the Federal Water Pollution Control Act (FWPCA) and was amended in 1977 as the CWA. The objective of the CWA (Sec. 101) is "to restore and maintain the chemical, physical, and biological integrity of the Nation's waters." The "waters" to which the objective refers are largely surface waters and not ground waters. Some protection of ground water is afforded by the Safe Drinking Water Act. The CWA provides for water quality standards (Sec. 303), for effluent standards (Sec. 301), for the listing and regulation of toxic pollutants (Sec. 307), for the listing and regulation of hazardous substances (Sec. 311), for the regulation of publicly owned treatment works (POTWs), for state certification that discharges under any CWA permit will not violate state water quality standards (Sec. 401), for NPDES permits (Sec. 402), and for dredged or fill material discharge permits (Sec. 404). The 1977 amendments established three categories of pollutants: toxic pollutants, including an initial list of 129 chemicals (Sec. 307(a)); conventional pollutants (Sec. 304(a)(4)); and nonconventional pollutants (Sec. 301(g)) which include ammonia, chlorine, color, iron, and total phenols. Conventional pollutants under the CWA include biological oxygen demand (BOD), suspended solids (SS), fecal coliform bacteria, and pH. BOD is the amount of oxygen necessary to decompose organic material in water. pH is the acidity of the water. Again, the CWA is directed mainly at surface waters. A waiver of sovereign immunity appears in Sec. 313.

Unlike the old CAA, where requirements were established to meet the NAAQSs, requirements under the CWA are directed at uniform discharge standards from both existing and new sources, even if the discharges do not result in violation of water quality standards.

EPA's Water Quality Regulations (40 CFR 100-140 and 400-501)

Federal regulations implementing the CWA appear in 40 CFR 100-140 and 400-501. Significant CWA regulations are discussed below.

40 CFR 116, "Designation of Hazardous Substances" (CWA Sec. 311)

EPA's regulations in 40 CFR 116 list approximately 300 hazardous substances regulated under the CWA. A hazardous substance is defined as one which, when discharged in any quantity into or upon the navigable waters of the United States or adjoining shore-lines, presents an imminent and substantial danger to the public health or welfare, including, but not limited to, fish, shellfish, wildlife, shorelines, and beaches (CWA Sec, 11(b)(2)(A)).

40 CFR 117, "Determination of Reportable Quantities for Hazardous Substances" (CWA Sec. 311)

EPA's regulations in 40 CFR 117 list reportable quantities for releases of hazardous substances, unless covered by an NPDES permit.

40 CFR 121, "State Certification of Activities Requiring a Federal License or Permit" (CWA Sec. 401)

These regulations provide for state certification that any activity requiring a federal permit, i.e., an NPDES permit or a discharge of dredged or fill material permit, will not violate state water quality standards.

40 CFR 122, "The National Pollutant Discharge Elimination System" (CWA Sec. 402)

EPA regulations in 40 CFR 122 (and also in 40 CFR 125 and 129) apply to the discharge of pollutants from point sources into waters of the United States. NPDES permits are required by 40 CFR 122 for new and existing sources. Pollutant means dredged spoil, solid waste, incinerator residue, filter backwash, sewage, garbage, sewage sludge, munitions, chemical wastes, biological materials, radioactive materials, heat, wrecked or discarded equipment, rock, sand, cellar dirt, and industrial, municipal, and agricultural waste discharged into water. However, the U.S. Supreme Court on June 1, 1976, held that "pollutants" subject to regulation under the CWA do not include source, by-product, or special nuclear materials in Train v. Colorado.

Note that pollutants include munitions. In 1982 the Navy, in Weinberger v. Romero-Barcelo, was required by the U.S. Supreme Court to obtain a permit for bombing practice off Puerto Rico because of munitions falling into coastal waters.

Section 316 of the CWA covers thermal discharges specifically and permits state regulation of thermal discharges.

EPA's NPDES permit requirements in 40 CFR 122, 123, and 124 have been extended to the discharge of storm water. These regulations cover the point source discharge of storm waters into waters of the United States from industrial plants, cities, and counties. Applicants can choose among general permits, group permits, and individual permits. Construction activities over 5 acres in area must have a permit. Parking lot runoff permits are not required unless runoff is also from an industrial activity.

Although radioactive materials are regulated under the CWA, those radioactive materials that are source, by-product, or special nuclear material are not regulated. The Atomic Energy Act (42 USC 2011) definitions of source, by-product, and special nuclear material are:

> "The term 'source material' means 1) uranium, thorium, or any other material which is determined by the Commission . . . to be source material; or 2) ores containing one or more of the foregoing materials, in such concentrations as the Commission may by regulation determine from time to time." "The term 'by-product material' means 1) any radioactive material (except special nuclear material) yielded in or made radioactive by exposure to the radiation incident to the process of producing or utilizing special nuclear material, and 2) the tailings or

wastes produced by the extraction or concentration of uranium or thorium from any ore processed primarily for its source material content." "The term 'special nuclear material' means 1) plutonium, uranium enriched in the isotope 233 or in the isotope 235, and any other material which the Commission . . . determines to be special nuclear material; or 2) any material artificially enriched by any of the foregoing, but does not include source material."

States can be delegated the authority by EPA to administer the NPDES program. States can also veto an EPA-issued NPDES permit under Sec. 401 of the CWA.

40 CFR 129, "Toxic Pollutant Effluent Standards" (CWA Sec. 307)

EPA regulations in 40 CFR 129 provide a short list of toxic organic pollutant subject to NPDES permits, including aldrin, DDT, and PCBs.

40 CFR 131, "Water Quality Standards" (CWA Sec. 303)

These regulations present the requirements for state development of water quality standards.

40 CFR 133, "Secondary Treatment Regulation"

Regulations in 40 CFR 133 prescribe the minimum level of effluent quality to be obtained by secondary treatment in POTWs (municipal sewage disposal plants) for BOD, SS, and pH.

40 CFR 230-233, Discharges of Dredged or Fill Material (CWA Sec. 404)

These regulations contain guidelines for COE permits (33 CFR 323) relating to the discharges of dredged or fill material into waters of the United States. The EPA has the authority to veto a COE Section 404 permit on environmental protection grounds. The Two Forks Dam permit was vetoed by EPA in 1990 because the dam would inundate wetlands, scenic areas, and trout habitat. The purpose of the dam was to provide increased water supplies for suburban Denver communities. States can be delegated authority to administer the Sec. 404 permit and can also veto a Section 404 permit issued by the COE under Section 401.

40 CFR 400-501, "Effluent Guidelines and Standards"

Regulations in 40 CFR 400-501 prescribe effluent limitations guidelines for existing sources, standards of performance for new sources, and pretreatment standards for new and existing sources. These are directed at a long list of various categories of industries.

Navigable Waters

The Clean Water Act in Section 502(7) states that, "The term 'navigable waters' means waters of the United States . . ." (33 USC 1362(7)). Yet the COE defines "navigable waters" and "waters of the United States" differently in its regulations. To the COE, "navigable waters" are waters that are used, have been used, or could be used to transport interstate or foreign commerce (33 CFR 329) and "waters of the United States" are almost any body of water including rivers, lakes, ponds, and prairie potholes (33 CFR 328). The difference lies in the COE's responsibilities under the Rivers and Harbors Act (33 CFR 329) and under the Clean Water Act (33 CFR 328). Thus, the COE's two important water quality environmental permits may apply to different bodies of water. These permits are the permit for the discharge of dredged or fill material (33 CFR 323) into waters of the United States under the Clean Water Act and the permit for structures or work in or affecting navigable waters of the United States (33 CFR 322) under the Rivers and Harbors Act. In general, the discharge of dredged or fill material permit applies to many more bodies of water than the permit for structures or work. See Chapter 24.

Chapter 13 — Oil Pollution Act

The Oil Pollution Act (33 USC 2701 et seq.) of 1990 is closely related to the CWA and was enacted following the Exxon Valdez oil spill in Alaska. It includes provisions for the cleanup of oil spills on navigable waters and shorelines and for natural resource damage assessments for oil spills (Sec. 1002(b) and 1006). The Oil Pollution Act (OPA) also contains provisions for improved safety of oil transport, for example, double hulls for tank vessels (Sec. 4115).

Reporting and removal of oil spills and spills of hazardous substances as defined under the CWA are required by Sec. 311 of the CWA. Also, reporting and removal of spills of hazardous substances as defined under CERCLA are required by Sections 103 and 104 of CERCLA, respectively. Furthermore, Section 107(f) of CERCLA provides for natural resource damage assessments for spills of CERCLA hazardous substances.

Because hazardous substances are defined both under the CWA and under CERCLA, because reporting of spills of hazardous substances is required under both the CWA and CERCLA, because cleanup of spills of hazardous substances is required under both the CWA and CERCLA, because the cleanup of oil spills is required under both the OPA and CWA, and because natural resource damage assessments are required under both the OPA and CERCLA, these three federal environmental laws are closely related and there can be overlap (and confusion) among the requirements. It all serves to make environmental law a bit painful for the student and a lot of fun for the observer!

The Safe Drinking Water Act (42 USC 300f et seq.) was enacted in 1974, was amended in 1986 and 1996, and provides for the regulation of public drinking water systems (Sec. 1411), for the establishment of national standards for levels of contaminants in drinking water (Sec. 1412), for the regulation of underground injection wells (Sec. 1421), for the identification of sole source aquifers (Sec. 1427), and for the state protection of wellhead areas (Sec. 1428). Under Sec. 1413, a state may be delegated primary enforcement responsibility by EPA for public drinking water systems. Sections 1421, 1427, and 1428 afford some protection of ground water, i.e., the SDWA applies to both surface and ground water. A waiver of sovereign immunity appears in Sec. 1447 of the SDWA. This waiver is with respect to federally owned or maintained public drinking water systems and with respect to federal underground injection activities that may endanger drinking water.

The SDWA amendments of 1996 provide for improved communication between operators of drinking water systems and customers concerning drinking water purity, specifically by requiring periodic notice to customers of contaminants in the water. The amendments provide funds for improving water treatment facilities and for protecting water sources from contamination. They eliminate the old requirement to establish regulations for 25 contaminants every three years and replace it with a requirement to examine five priority contaminants every five years to determine whether or not regulation is warranted.

EPA's SDWA Regulations (40 CFR 141-149)

EPA's safe drinking water standards appear in 40 CFR 141-149. Significant regulations are discussed below.

40 CFR 141, "National Primary Drinking Water Regulations" (SDWA Sec. 1412)

EPA's drinking water standards in 40 CFR 141 are called maximum contaminant levels and maximum contaminant level goals and apply to community water systems. Regulations now exist for a substantial list of contaminants that includes organic compounds, inorganic compounds, heavy metal ions, radionuclides, bacteria, and turbidity. For example, standards exist for asbestos, As, Ba, Cd, Cr, Hg, nitrate, Se, vinyl chloride, benzene, carbon tetrachloride, trichloroethylene, etc. Radioactivity standards are set at 4 mrem/yr. These regulations are of major importance as cleanup standards (applicable or relevant and appropriate requirements or ARARs) under CERCLA.

40 CFR 144-147, "Underground Injection Control Program" (SDWA Sec. 1421)

EPA regulations in 40 CFR 144-147 apply to the underground injection of liquids and wastes and may require a permit for any underground injection. The regulations include definitions for five different classes of injection wells. The definition of underground sources of drinking water (USDW) appears in Sec. 144.3.

40 CFR 149, "Sole Source Aquifers" (SDWA Sec. 1427)

EPA's regulations in 40 CFR 149 provide criteria for the identification of sole source aquifers (for drinking water). As of 1992, EPA had designated approximately 50 sole source aquifers. A sole source aquifer can consist of a large geographic area that, once designated, would not be eligible for federal funds for any activity that might contaminate the aquifer.

Sole source aquifers can become substantial land-use issues because wide areas may be involved. However, if EPA is the only federal agency involved, then the possibility exists that no EIS will be prepared for public disclosure and comment and that all of the public participation will be conducted under EPA's SDWA regulations rather than under NEPA. Wellhead protection usually involves smaller land areas around a given well or small set of wells and thus need not become a major issue.

Chapter 15

Resource Conservation and Recovery Act

RCRA (42 USC 6901 et seq.) was passed in 1976 as an amendment to the Solid Waste Disposal Act (enacted in 1965) and amended in 1984 by the Hazardous and Solid Waste Amendments. The purpose of RCRA is to reduce or eliminate the generation of hazardous waste and to treat, store, and dispose of hazardous waste to minimize the present and future threat to human health and the environment (Sec. 1003). RCRA is a "cradle-to-grave" system for managing hazardous waste that applies mainly to active facilities and that requires a manifest system for the generation, transport, treatment, storage, and disposal of hazardous wastes and requires permits for the treatment, storage, or disposal of hazardous wastes (Subtitle C, Sections 3001-3019) (Figure 6). HSWA institutes a land disposal ban program and a corrective action program. In addition, Subtitle C provides for ground water protection from the TSD of hazardous wastes, and Subtitle I provides for the regulation of underground storage tanks containing regulated substances, i.e., petroleum and CERCLA hazardous substances other than RCRA hazardous wastes. Hazardous wastes in tanks are regulated under Subtitle C of RCRA. RCRA is administered either by the EPA or by the states when delegated by EPA. Sec. 3001 provides for identifying and either "listing" or "characterizing" (ignitable, toxic, corrosive, reactive) hazardous wastes. Sec. 3002 requires generators of hazardous wastes to prepare manifests to track the generation, transport, treatment, storage, and disposal of the generated wastes. Sec. 3003 requires transporters of hazardous wastes to meet RCRA transportation requirements as well as those in the Hazardous Materials Transportation Act (49 USC 1801 et seq.) and in the Department of Transportation's Hazardous Waste Transportation regulations in 49 CFR 171-179. Sec. 3004

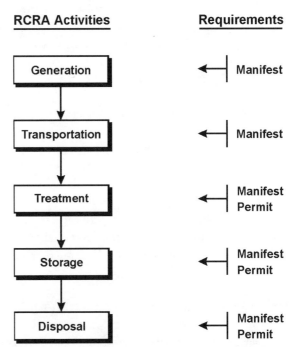

Figure 6. RCRA flow chart. All RCRA activities require a manifest that accompanies the waste from its creation to final disposal. Treatment, storage, and/or disposal of hazardous wastes require a permit.

requires the owners and operators of TSD facilities to comply with performance standards, groundwater monitoring requirements, and land-ban requirements prohibiting the disposal of untreated hazardous wastes in landfills. Sec. 3005 requires the owners and operators of TSD facilities to obtain RCRA permits and establishes "interim status" for facilities in existence before November 19, 1980. Sec. 3006 provides for state administration of the RCRA program. Subtitle D provides for "State or Regional Solid Waste Plans," i.e., for the regulation of garbage. Subtitle J provides for a two-year demonstration program for the tracking of medical wastes. A waiver of sovereign immunity appears in Sec. 6001.

The RCRA definitions of "solid waste" and "hazardous waste" are central to an understanding of the statute and are to be distinguished from similar definitions in other statutes, for example "hazardous substance," "pollutant," or "contaminant" in CERCLA and "pollutant" or "hazardous substance" in the CWA.

> The term "solid waste" means any garbage, refuse, sludge, from a waste treatment plant or air pollution control facility and other discarded material, including solid, liquid, semisolid, or contained gaseous materials resulting from industrial, commercial, mining and agricultural activities and from community activities but does not include solid or dissolved material in domestic sewage, or solid or dissolved materials in irrigation return flows or industrial discharges which are point sources subject to permits under Sec. 402 of the Federal Water Pollution Control Act, as amended, or source, special nuclear, or by-product material as defined by the Atomic Energy Act of 1954 as amended (RCRA Sec. 1004(27)).

It is important to note that, under RCRA, liquids can be solid wastes.

> The term "hazardous waste" means a solid waste, or combination of solid wastes, which because of its quantity, concentration, or physical, chemical, or infectious characteristics may—(A) cause, or significantly contribute to an increase in mortality or an increase in serious irreversible, or incapacitating reversible, illness, or (B) pose a substantial present or potential hazard to human health or the environment when improperly treated, stored, transported, or disposed of, or otherwise managed.

Wastes that are exempted from RCRA regulation are regulated elsewhere, are exempted by the law itself, or are exempted in the RCRA regulations. These include domestic sewage, effluents regulated under the CWA; source, by-product, and special nuclear material; irrigation return flows; household wastes; coal combustion wastes (flyash waste, bottom ash waste, slag waste, and flue gas emission control waste); drilling muds and brine used in oil, gas, and geothermal operations; mining wastes from extraction, treatment, and processing of ores and minerals; cement kiln dust; and wastes produced by small quantity generators (RCRA Sec. 3001 and 40 CFR 261.4).

The 1984 amendments (HSWA) shifted emphasis on the management of hazardous wastes from land disposal to treatment alternatives (see 40 CFR 268)).

EPA's Hazardous Waste Regulations in 40 CFR 260-281

EPA's RCRA (hazardous waste management) regulations appear in 40 CFR 260-272. They apply to the generation, transport, treatment, storage, and disposal of hazardous wastes, but not to source, by-product, or special nuclear material, i.e., not in general to radioactive wastes. They also apply to the hazardous component of hazardous and radioactive mixed wastes, but not to the radioactive component. RCRA permits may be required by these regulations.

40 CFR 261, "Identification and Listing of Hazardous Waste"

40 CFR 261 defines and presents lists of hazardous wastes. Wastes include both "listed" wastes (listed in 40 CFR 261) and "characteristic" wastes (defined in 40 CFR 261). Characteristic wastes are those that are ignitable, corrosive, reactive, or toxic. The toxicity characteristic leaching procedure (TCLP), which defines toxicity, appears in 40 CFR 261. Listed wastes are listed by name or by designation of a specific waste stream. Characteristic wastes are not identified by name, but are identified by their chemical properties, except that toxic wastes are identified by failing the TCLP. In this test, the waste form is leached with acetic acid and is designated a toxic waste if certain chemical elements or compounds, such as some heavy metals or chlorinated organic compounds, appear in the leachate in concentrations greater than those designated in the regulations.

40 CFR 262, "Standards Applicable to Generators of Hazardous Waste"

Regulations in 40 CFR 262 require EPA identification numbers for generators of hazardous waste and require manifesting and record keeping procedures.

40 CFR 263, "Standards Applicable to Transporters of Hazardous Waste"

Regulations in 40 CFR 263 apply to transporters (both inter- and intrastate) of hazardous wastes and require continued record keeping, as well as compliance with the DOT's hazardous materials transportation regulations in 49 CFR 171-179.

40 CFR 264, "Standards for Owners and Operators of Hazardous Waste Treatment, Storage, and Disposal Facilities"

Standards in 40 CFR 264 apply to owners and operators of TSD facilities that have RCRA Part B permits (permitted facilities). Facilities covered include containers, tank systems, surface impoundments, waste piles, land treatment facilities, landfills, incinerators, and miscellaneous units. Operation, closure, and post-closure periods are covered. The regulations nominally contemplate a 30-year post-closure period (during which time the owner/operator of a TSD facility may not be receiving any income from the facility). Monitoring requirements, ground water protection requirements, and corrective action requirements are specified. Corrective action is required whenever hazardous wastes are released or found to be migrating from a RCRA facility. If the owner/operator of the TSD facility wishes to continue operating the facility, then corrective action requirements will be a condition of operation and may be made part of the TSD permit.

40 CFR 265, "Interim Standards for Owners and Operators of Hazardous Waste Treatment, Storage, and Disposal Facilities"

Standards in 40 CFR 265 apply to owners and operators of essentially the same hazardous waste facilities as those covered in 40 CFR 264, as well as thermal treatment units, chemical, physical, and biological treatment units, and underground injection wells, but not miscellaneous units, except that the facilities have interim status and do not have a RCRA permit (interim status facilities). Interim status applies to existing facilities and was generally attained by filing a Part A permit application for facilities existing on November 19, 1980.

40 CFR 268, "Land Disposal Restrictions"

40 CFR 268 covers land disposal restrictions which, in general, prohibit land disposal of many hazardous wastes unless the wastes have been treated prior to disposal, or unless it can be shown that the wastes will not migrate. Treatment technologies are prescribed in the regulations.

40 CFR 270-272, RCRA permit program

The regulations in 40 CFR 270-272 describe the RCRA permit program and state authorization to conduct the RCRA program.

EPA's Underground Storage Tank Regulations in 40 CFR 280-282

EPA regulations in 40 CFR 280-282 apply to underground storage tanks containing regulated substances (not hazardous wastes). A regulated substance includes petroleum and any hazardous substance regulated under CERCLA, but not any hazardous waste regulated under Subtitle C of RCRA. EPA may authorize state regulation of underground storage tanks (and a state permit).

Other Solid Waste Regulations

EPA's regulations in 40 CFR 240-259, Guidelines for the Management of Solid Wastes, provide guidelines and minimum national criteria for the state management of municipal solid waste landfills.

EPA regulations in 40 CFR 279, Standards for the Management of Used Oil, apply to the handling of used and recycled oil. They apply specifically to generators, transporters, and processors of oil, to the burning of oil for energy, and to the use of oil as a dust suppressant.

Chapter 16　Federal Facility Compliance Act

The Federal Facility Compliance Act is an amendment to RCRA that broadens the waiver of sovereign immunity under RCRA and provides for state fines against the federal government for violations of RCRA, although federal employees are not personally liable for civil violations. The FFCA speaks specifically to mixed wastes owned by the federal government and requires agencies of the federal government to prepare an inventory of mixed wastes, an inventory of treatment methods, and a plan for managing and disposing of mixed wastes. Mixed wastes are presently stored and not disposed.

Chapter 17 Pollution Prevention Act

The Pollution Prevention Act of 1990 (42 USC 13101 et seq.) provides for the development of strategies by EPA to reduce pollution by reduction of the sources of pollution.

CERCLA (42 USC 9601 et seq.), passed in 1980 and amended by the Superfund Amendments and Reauthorization Act in 1986, provides for remedial action at inactive or abandoned waste sites (cleanup), provides for removal action (also cleanup) of spills of oil and hazardous substances, provides for reporting any release to the environment of a hazardous substance, and provides for natural resource damage assessments. CERCLA, in general, is directed at the protection of human health (Sec. 121(b)) and provides a remedial action program for past hazardous waste activities, while RCRA provides a regulatory program for present hazardous waste activities. CERCLA Section 107 provides for the payment of monetary damages for injury, destruction, or loss caused to natural resources caused by releases of hazardous substances to the environment (natural resource damage assessments, or NRDA). A waiver of sovereign immunity appears in Sec. 120 of CERCLA.

The environment under CERCLA includes air, any surface water, ground water, land surface, and subsurface strata, but not biota (CERCLA Sec. 101(8)). CERCLA is triggered by the release or substantial threat of release of any "hazardous substance" into the environment, or the release or threat of release into the environment of any "pollutant" or "contaminant" that may present an imminent and substantial danger to the public health or welfare (CERCLA Sec. 104). "Hazardous substance" is defined as any substance regulated under the CAA Sec. 112, CWA Sec. 311(b)(2)(A) (hazardous substances) or 307(a) (toxic pollutants), TSCA Sec. 7, and RCRA Sec. 3001 (CERCLA Sec. 101 (14)), except that petroleum and natural gas are specifically excluded from the definition of hazardous substance. The complete list of hazardous substances appears in 40 CFR 302. Petroleum spills are regulated under Sec. 311(c) of the CWA and under the Oil Pollution Act of 1990. However, oil spill cleanup (removal) requirements are included under the CERCLA regulations in 40 CFR 300. "Pollutant or contaminant" means any substance likely to cause death, disease, abnormalities, etc. (CERCLA Sec. 101 (33)). Note that RCRA is triggered by "wastes," while CERCLA is triggered by any "hazardous substance." Both "removal" actions and "remedial" actions are provided for under CERCLA. Removal actions refer to spills requiring immediate action, while remedial actions refer to longer term cleanup of inactive sites. No permits are required for CERCLA cleanup activities conducted entirely on site. However, should any hazardous wastes be removed from a CERCLA site and placed elsewhere, then appropriate RCRA requirements must be followed including the acquisition of RCRA TSD permits. Radionuclides are regulated under CERCLA because they are hazardous air pollutants under Sec. 112 of the CAA (40 CFR 61).

EPA's Hazardous Substance Cleanup Regulations in 40 CFR 300-302

Significant CERCLA regulations are discussed below.

40 CFR 300, "National Oil and Hazardous Substances Pollution Contingency Plan"

EPA's CERCLA regulations in 40 CFR 300 apply to the cleanup of discharges of oil and releases of hazardous substances into the environment and, in particular, to the cleanup of inactive or abandoned hazardous waste disposal sites. 40 CFR 300 is the so-called "National Contingency Plan" (NCP) which provides for the development of a "National Priorities List" (NPL) of sites for which cleanup is mandated. Placement on the NPL triggers the RI/FS process, which includes an RI/FS work plan, a remedial investigation of the site and the status of the site's releases or threatened releases (including a risk assessment), and a feasibility study (engineering evaluation) of cleanup methods. The last step of the study is a record of decision (ROD), which records the cleanup method and the extent of cleanup (how clean is clean), which is dictated by the applicable or relevant and appropriate requirements (ARARs). Some states require cleanup to background levels. The CERCLA ROD is not the same as the EIS ROD. Following the ROD, remedial design and remedial action (RD/RA) are carried out, i.e., cleanup begins (and may continue for years). The NCP also contains provisions for the cleanup of oil spills under the CWA and OPA.

40 CFR 300.600-300.615, Natural Resource Damage Assessments

EPA's NRDA regulations appear in 40 CFR 300.600-300.615.

40 CFR 302, "Designation, Reportable Quantities, and Notification"

The EPA regulations in 40 CFR 302 list hazardous substances under CERCLA and list the quantities of hazardous substances that must be reported if released to the environment.

Applicable or Relevant and Appropriate Requirements

CERCLA does not contain specific cleanup standards for sites undergoing remedial action. Rather, CERCLA provides for "applicable or relevant and appropriate requirements" (CERCLA Sec. 121). These requirements include any environmental standard promulgated under state or federal law, including especially the MCLGs promulgated in 40 CFR 141 under the SDWA. Standards exist for air and water, but few standards exist for soil cleanup. States, however, are beginning to adopt soil cleanup standards that will serve as ARARs.

ARARs are important in an EIS if the subject of the EIS is a cleanup project or if the EIS involves meeting CERCLA requirements. This is because the CERCLA requirements may become mitigation actions in the EIS.

Learned papers have been written on the difference between "applicable" and "relevant and appropriate." This may be because the phrases "legally applicable," "relevant and appropriate," and "legally applicable or relevant and appropriate" are used separately in Sec. 121 of CERCLA, but are not defined in CERCLA. However, "applicable requirements" and "relevant and appropriate requirements" are defined separately in the

CERCLA regulations (40 CFR 300.5). For practical purposes, these differences are in the eyes of legal scholars. The differences need not cause problems for the writer of an EIS who must consider all state or federally promulgated environmental standards as potential ARARs for CERCLA cleanup activities.

Federal Facility Compliance Agreements

A number of federal agencies, particularly the Department of Energy, have entered into compliance agreements and consent orders with the EPA and the involved state for the cleanup of federal sites owned by these agencies. The agreements are thought to be legally enforceable and have usually been written after the site has been placed on the National Priorities List. They often extend for many years into the future and may be very detailed. Fortunately, they may be amended. Unfortunately, Congress is not bound by these agreements and may or may not appropriate the money to carry out the agreement.

An example is the "Federal Facility Agreement and Consent Order," among the DOE, EPA, and the Washington Department of Ecology, for the cleanup of the Hanford Site in southeastern Washington.[1] This agreement was signed in 1989, nominally extends for thirty years, and has been amended several times.

REFERENCE

(1)   "Hanford Federal Facility Agreement and Compliance Order," Washington Department of Ecology, U.S. Environmental Protection Agency and U.S. Department of Energy, May 1989, as amended.

Chapter 19 — Hazardous Materials Transportation Act

The Hazardous Materials Transportation Act (49 USC 1801 et seq.) provides for the regulation of the transport of hazardous materials by the Department of Transportation (DOT). Close coordination between the DOT and EPA is required under RCRA (Sec. 3003) for the transportation of hazardous wastes.

DOT's Hazardous Materials Transportation Regulations in 49 CFR 171-179

The Department of Transportation regulations in 49 CFR 171-179, "Hazardous Materials Regulations," promulgated under the Hazardous Materials Transportation Act, apply to the handling, packaging, labeling, and shipment of hazardous materials, including hazardous and radioactive wastes.

Chapter 20 | Toxic Substances Control Act

The Toxic Substances Control Act (15 USC 2601 et seq.) provides for the testing and regulation of chemical substances, particularly new substances, entering the environment. EPA may regulate the manufacture, use, distribution, and disposal of these substances. Manufacturers must notify the EPA before producing a new chemical substance, at which time the EPA can require testing before the substance enters the environment. If a chemical substance poses an unusual risk, the EPA may restrict its manufacture and use. The Toxic Substances Control Act (TSCA) supplements the CAA and the CWA and applies to chemicals that are not necessarily considered to be wastes.

Sections 201-215 of TSCA cover asbestos in schools and in public and commercial buildings. Asbestos is also regulated under the CAA in 40 CFR 61. Sections 301-311 cover indoor radon abatement.

EPA's TSCA Regulations in 40 CFR 700-799

EPA's regulations in 40 CFR 700-799 implement TSCA and, in particular, regulate polychlorinated biphenyls (PCBs), asbestos, and dioxins. PCBs are covered in 40 CFR 761, asbestos in 40 CFR 763 (see also 40 CFR 61), and dioxins in 40 CFR 766. Cleanup standards for PCBs in soil appear in 40 CFR 761.

Chapter 21 Species Protection Acts

Significant federal species protection acts include the Endangered Species Act (16 USC 1531 et seq.), the Fish and Wildlife Coordination Act (16 USC 661 et seq.), the Bald and Golden Eagle Protection Act (16 USC 668 et seq.), and the Migratory Bird Treaty Act (16 USC 703 et seq.). Depending on the scope of the EIS, attention to the requirements of these acts may be necessary in the EIS.

Endangered Species Act

The Endangered Species Act provides for the protection of plant and animal species listed by the U.S. Fish and Wildlife Service or the National Marine Fisheries Service as "threatened" or "endangered." "Critical habitat" for threatened or endangered species, which also enjoys special protection, may be designated by these agencies. A formal biological assessment may be required for any project that might impact threatened or endangered species. A less formal biological survey should be carried out for any EIS that involves land use.

Fish and Wildlife Coordination Act

The Fish and Wildlife Coordination Act provides habitat protection by requiring any federal agency to consult with the U.S. Fish and Wildlife Service whenever the agency proposes to impound, divert, deepen, or otherwise control or modify a stream or other body of water. The purpose of this consultation is to assure conservation of wildlife resources by preventing loss of or damage to habitat.

Bald and Golden Eagle Protection Act

The Bald and Golden Eagle Protection Act provides for the protection of bald and golden eagles by prohibiting the "taking" of these species by pursuing, wounding, killing, capturing, molesting, or disturbing the eagles, nests, or eggs.

Migratory Bird Treaty Act

The Migratory Bird Treaty Act provides for the protection of migratory birds that are included in treaties among the United States, Great Britain, Mexico, and Japan.

Species Protection Regulations

Regulations of the Endangered Species Act, the Bald and Golden Eagle Protection Act, and the Migratory Bird Treaty Act appear in 50 CFR 10-24 and 50 CFR 402 and apply to the protection of these species. Other species protection regulations appear in 50 CFR 216-229, 424, and 450-453.

Historic, scenic, aesthetic, and cultural preservation acts include the National Historic Preservation Act (16 USC 470-470w-6), the Archaeological Resources Protection Act (16 USC 470aa-470ll), the Archaeological and Historic Preservation Act (16 USC 469-469c), the American Antiquities Act (16 USC 431-433), the American Indian Religious Freedom Act (42 USC 1996), the Native American Graves Protection and Repatriation Act (25 USC 3001 et seq.), and the Wild and Scenic Rivers Act (16 USC 1274 et seq.).

National Historic Preservation Act

The National Historic Preservation Act provides for the listing of historic properties and sites in the National Register of Historic Places and provides for the protection of these properties and sites. The act provides for a state historic preservation officer (SHPO) with whom consultation is required on matters relating to properties or sites that are either on the National Register or that are potentially eligible for listing on the National Register.

Archaeological Resources Protection Act, Archaeological and Historic Preservation Act, and American Antiquities Act

These acts provide for the protection of archaeological and paleontological resources on public and Indian lands and for protection of similar resources during dam construction.

American Indian Religious Freedom Act

The American Indian Religious Freedom Act establishes the United States' policy to protect and preserve for American Indians their inherent right of freedom to believe, express, and exercise their traditional religions, including access to sites, use and possession of sacred objects, and the freedom to worship through ceremonies and traditional rites.

Native American Graves Protection and Repatriation Act

The Native American Graves Protection and Repatriation Act provides that tribal descendants shall own Native American human remains and cultural items discovered on federal lands after November 16, 1990.

Wild and Scenic Rivers Act

The Wild and Scenic Rivers Act provides for the listing by Congress of rivers and streams as wild, scenic, or recreational rivers and for the protection of these streams and adjacent areas from development.

Historic, Scenic, and Cultural Preservation Regulations

Historic, scenic, and cultural preservation requirements appear in several places in the CFR. The regulations include those that implement the National Historic Preservation Act in 36 CFR 800 (Protection of Historic and Cultural Properties), 36 CFR 18 (Leases and Exchanges of Historic Property), 36 CFR 60 (National Register of Historic Places), 36 CFR 63 (Determination of Eligibility for Inclusion in the National Register of Historic Places), and 36 CFR 79 (Curation of Federally Owned and Administered Archaeological Collections); the American Antiquities Act in 25 CFR 261 and 43 CFR 3; the Archaeological Resources Protection Act and the American Indian Religious Freedom Act in 36 CFR 296 and 43 CFR 7; and the Native American Graves Protection and Repatriation Act in 43 CFR 10. These regulations apply to the protection of historic and cultural properties, including both existing properties and those discovered during excavation and construction. The SHPO has been delegated substantial authority under federal law for local administration of historic preservation. Consultation with the SHPO is appropriate in the preparation of any EIS involving both developed and undeveloped land.

Indian Treaties

Federal facilities are sometimes located on lands ceded by Indian tribes to the federal government. These treaties frequently provide specific rights to the tribes above and beyond those in the American Indian Religious Freedom Act, the Native American Graves Protection and Repatriation Act, and the other historic preservation acts. These treaty rights have not always been honored in the past, but should be specifically recognized in any federal EIS involving ceded lands.

Chapter 23

Nuclear Materials and Nuclear Waste Handling Acts

The Atomic Energy Act (AEA) (42 USC 2011 et seq.), the Low-Level Radioactive Waste Policy Act (LLRWPA) (42 USC 2021b et seq.), and the Nuclear Waste Policy Act (NWPA) (42 USC 10101 et seq.), while not environmental laws per se, contain provisions under which environmental regulations applicable to radioactive materials may be or have been promulgated.

The AEA and subsequent amendments provide for the Department of Energy to manage radioactive materials owned by the federal government, specifically source, by-product, and special nuclear material, and provide for the Nuclear Regulatory Commission to regulate civilian uses of radioactive materials. These uses include electric power production and the production and use of medical isotopes in commercial facilities. Regulatory authority is shared by the NRC with some states (agreement states) for some commercial uses of radioactive material.

The LLRWPA provides for the creation of state compacts for locating and operating commercial low-level radioactive waste burial grounds. While compacts have been formed, little progress has been made in siting and constructing actual burial grounds.

The NWPA provides for the federal government to construct and operate a repository for commercial spent nuclear fuel and for some federally owned spent nuclear fuel and high-level nuclear waste. A repository at Yucca Mountain, Nevada, is under study, but continued scientific and political controversies have prevented major construction activities.

Radioactive Materials and Radioactive Waste Management Regulations

Significant radioactive materials and radioactive waste management regulations include the following:

40 CFR 190, "Environmental Radiation Protection Standards for Nuclear Power Operations"

EPA regulations in 40 CFR 190 apply to radiation doses to the public from commercial nuclear fuel cycle activities.

40 CFR 191, "Environmental Radiation Protection Standards for Management and Disposal of Spent Nuclear Fuel, High-Level and Transuranic Radioactive Wastes"

EPA regulations in 40 CFR 191 provide environmental standards for the management, storage, and disposal of spent nuclear fuel, high-level radioactive wastes, and transuranic radioactive wastes.

10 CFR 0-199, U.S. Nuclear Regulatory Commission Regulations

The NRC regulations in 10 CFR 0-199 apply to radioactive materials and nuclear facilities owned by commercial establishments. Regulations include 10 CFR 20 "Standards for Protection against Radiation," 10 CFR 50 "Domestic Licensing of Production and Utilization Facilities" (commercial reactors), 10 CFR 51 "Environmental Protection Regulations for Domestic Licensing and Related Regulatory Functions" (NRC's EIS regulations), 10 CFR 60 "Disposal of High-Level Radioactive Wastes in Geologic Repositories," and 10 CFR 61 "Licensing Requirements for Land Disposal of Radioactive Waste." The NRC regulations in 10 CFR 60 are consistent with the EPA regulations in 40 CFR 191.

Chapter 24 | Other Significant Environmental Regulations

Other significant environmental regulations include permits for structures or work in or affecting navigable waters of the United States and for discharges of dredged or fill material into waters of the United States.

Structures or Work

33 CFR 322, "Permits for Structures or Work in or Affecting Navigable Waters of the United States"

Structures and work in navigable waters require a COE permit under Section 10 of the Rivers and Harbors Act of 1899. Navigable waters are defined by the COE in 33 CFR 329.

Discharges

33 CFR 323, "Permits for Discharges of Dredged or Fill Material into Waters of the United States"

The discharge of dredged or fill material into waters of the United States requires a COE permit under Section 404 of the CWA. The EPA has the authority to veto a Section 404 permit on environmental protection grounds (40 CFR 230-233). States, as well, can veto Sec. 404 permits (and also NPDES permits) on the grounds that the discharges would violate state water quality standards. Waters of the United States are defined by the COE in 33 CFR 328.

Chapter 25   Environmental Permits

Major federal environmental permits are listed below. These permits may be administered either by a federal agency or by a state agency depending upon whether or not the state has received federal approval to issue the permit. Furthermore, all of these permits apply to federal agencies and, again depending on federal approval, may be administered by the states.

CAA: PSD permit (40 CFR 52 and 70)

CAA: NESHAP authorization (40 CFR 61, 63, and 70)

CAA: New or modified major source in a nonattainment area
               (40 CFR 52 and 70)

CAA: After 1990, a single air quality permit
               (40 CFR 70 and 71)

CWA: NPDES permit (40 CFR 122)

SDWA: UIC permit (40 CFR 144)

CWA: COE dredged or fill permit (33 CFR 323, 33 CFR 328, and
               40 CFR 230-233

RCRA: RCRA TSD permit (40 CFR 264-265)

RCRA: UST permit (40 CFR 280-281)

RHA: COE structures or work in waters permit (33 CFR 322,
               33 CF 329))

Chapter 26 — Numerical Standards for Protection of the Public

Numerical standards for protecting the public from releases to the environment have been set by the EPA and appear in air quality, water quality, solid waste, and radioactivity regulations. These standards are important as ARARs under CERCLA, and as requirements for protection of the public and for mitigation in an EIS. Some examples are presented here.

Air Quality

40 CFR 50, "National Primary and Secondary Ambient Air Quality Standards"

The regulations in 40 CFR 50 set ambient air quality standards for air pollutants including oxides of nitrogen, particulates, carbon monoxide, sulfur dioxide, lead, and ozone. These standards are not directly enforceable, but provide the bases for other enforceable regulations and standards.

40 CFR 61, "National Emission Standards for Hazardous Air Pollutants"

EPA's standards in 40 CFR 61 apply to the release of hazardous substances to the atmosphere including arsenic, asbestos, benzene, beryllium, mercury, vinyl chloride, and some radionuclides. For example, the standards in 40 CFR 61.92 apply to releases of radionuclides to the atmosphere from DOE facilities:

> Emissions of radionuclides [other than radon 220 and 222] to the ambient air from Department of Energy facilities shall not exceed those amounts that would cause any member of the public to receive in any year an effective dose equivalent of 10 mrem/yr.

40 CFR 63, "National Emission Standards for Hazardous Air Pollutants for Source Categories"

EPA's standards in 40 CFR 63 apply to hazardous air pollutants listed in Section 112 of the Clean Air Act Amendments of 1990. The regulations are arranged by source categories.

Water Quality

40 CFR 141, "National Primary Drinking Water Standards"

EPA's standards in 40 CFR 141 apply indirectly to releases of radionuclides and hazardous substances into water to the extent that the releases impact community water systems. For example:

> The average annual concentration of beta particle and photon radioactivity from man-made radionuclides in drinking water shall not produce an annual dose equivalent to the body or any internal organ greater than 4 millirem/year (20,000 pCi/L for H-3, 8 pCi/L for Sr-90).

40 CFR 141 also specifies maximum concentrations for a growing list of chemical contaminants in drinking water. The limit, for example, of nitrate as nitrogen is 10 mg/L.

Environmental Radiation

40 CFR 190, "Environmental Radiation Standards for Nuclear Power Operations"

EPA's standards in 40 CFR 190 specify that "The annual dose equivalent [shall] not exceed 25 millirems to the whole body, 75 millirems to the thyroid, and 25 millirems to any other organ of any member of the public as a result of exposures to planned discharges of radioactive materials, radon and its daughters excepted, to the general environment from uranium fuel cycle operations and to radiation from these operations."

Hazardous Waste

40 CFR 264, "Standards for Owners and Operators of Hazardous Waste Treatment, Storage, and Disposal Systems"

EPA standards in 40 CFR 264 contain numerical standards for protecting the public from releases of hazardous wastes from hazardous waste disposal sites.

Chapter 27 — Penalties for Violations of Environmental Laws

Most federal environmental laws now contain penalties for violations of the law. And while these penalties are not of particular interest to the writer of an EIS, the existence of the penalties should be known to the environmental science student. Administrative, civil, and criminal penalties are available against corporations, state and federal agencies, and individuals, including employees of state and federal agencies. An administrative penalty is a fine levied by a state or federal agency that can be appealed to a court. A civil penalty is a fine levied by a court against a company or an individual, which can include both compensatory damages and punitive damages. A criminal penalty is a court-ordered fine for an organization (company, government agency, etc.) or a fine and/or a jail sentence for an individual. Penalties can include an order to cease some activity or to carry out some activity. Both civil and criminal penalties are available for violations of the CAA, CWA, CERCLA, RCRA, TSCA, and SDWA. Details differ in each law.

Chapter 28 The EIS Public Hearing

Public meetings or public hearings are conducted during scoping of the EIS and following publication of the draft EIS. Scoping meetings are conducted for the purpose of assisting the lead agency in determining the actions, alternatives, and impacts to be considered in the EIS. Public hearings on the draft EIS are conducted for the purpose of securing comments on the draft EIS. In this chapter arrangements are discussed for conducting a public hearing on the draft EIS. Arrangements for scoping meetings can be inferred from those for the draft EIS.

Prehearing Arrangements

The first thing that must be done in preparing for a public hearing is to select the times and places for the hearing. A public hearing of limited local interest need only be held in one town or city near the proposed action. If there are other locations involved in the alternatives, then a public hearing should be held in each location. A linear facility such as a highway or high voltage transmission line may require several hearings along the route. A public hearing can be held in a government building, a school, or a hotel/motel. A public hearing held in a public building is often less expensive than one held in a motel; but a motel will offer other services, such as room accommodations for those who must stay overnight, eating facilities, and easy access to telephones. Places should be selected with good parking, with reasonable access to public transportation, and with access for handicapped persons. Frequently, a public hearing in a given location will be held in two separate sessions during a single day to accommodate working and family schedules of interested persons. The format of each session will be the same. If it is desired to hold public information meetings in advance of the public hearings, then the times and locations of these meetings should be selected at the same time that the times and locations of the public hearings are selected.

After the times and places of the public hearings (and of the public information meetings, if any) are selected, the lead agency can announce in the *Federal Register* that the draft EIS has been published (notice of availability). This announcement will include the times and places of the hearings and of any public information meetings.

Before the hearings begin, display advertising should be placed in newspapers of general circulation near the hearing locations and, as appropriate, ads should be placed on local radio and television stations. Publication of this information in the *Federal Register* is never enough. Materials for display at the public information meetings (or at the hearings themselves, outside the hearing room) should be prepared at this time.

The hearing officer should also be selected early enough to give him or her the necessary time to prepare for the hearings. Ideally, the hearing officer will be a senior staff member of the lead agency with direct responsibility for the EIS.

At the Hearing

Personnel

Necessary personnel include the hearing officer, court reporter, someone outside the hearing room to take reservations to speak, an operator for the public address system, and agency personnel to answer questions and explain the displays (outside the hearing room). Security personnel should not be necessary.

Materials

Copies of the summary of the EIS should be available to all interested persons at the hearing. A few display copies of the EIS should also be available. The agency should also provide request forms for copies of the draft and/or final EIS. And, of course, appropriate displays should be present and available for public inspection.

Hearing Room Arrangement

If possible, a room should be selected for the public hearing that slopes downward toward the hearing officer and court reporter. This arrangement is less intimidating than one in which the public looks up at a stage. Sometimes only a level room is available, in which case a one-step riser may be necessary for visibility. A lectern should be provided for the speakers. A good public address system is a necessity.

Conduct of the Hearing

Public hearings on an EIS are conducted as legislative type hearings rather than as judicial hearings. Each person is allowed five minutes (or ten, if time is available) to speak, cross examination is not permitted, and the speakers need not be sworn in. The wise hearing officer will not contest or correct inaccurate statements by the speaker, but will let the agency do that in its responses to comments in the final EIS. The wise hearing officer will also encourage speakers to speak to the subject of the EIS, but will refrain from stopping speakers who are completely off the subject. He or she will only enforce the time limits. At the beginning of the hearing, the hearing officer will make certain statements for the record, including the title of the EIS, the lead and cooperating agencies, the date of publication in the *Federal Register* of the notice of intent and notice of availability, the procedures to be followed in the hearing, and the agency's process for responding to comments in the final EIS. After asking if there are questions on the procedure, the hearing officer will begin the hearing by calling on those who have preregistered in order. An elected official should be offered a time-certain to speak. This is a courtesy in deference to the office, not to the person. Persons who speak at public hearings should be encouraged (in advance) to prepare and submit written remarks. These become exhibits at the public hearing that the hearing officer should mark and preserve for the lead agency.

While security personnel should not be necessary at a public hearing on a draft EIS, unruly behavior cannot be tolerated. Simply recessing the hearing is usually enough to calm troubled waters. Any demonstrators with signs can be invited into the hearing room, asked to place their signs around the walls of the room where they can be seen, and invited to present comments on the EIS. Carrying signs into the seating area is not appropriate.

A verbatim record of the hearing is kept by the court reporter. Written transcripts of the record are placed in public information reading rooms by the lead agency as soon as the transcripts are available, along with the draft EIS itself and other documents related to the EIS.

Chapter 29 — Conclusion

In the past thirty years, consideration by federal agencies on the environmental impacts of their projects has progressed from no consideration at all in some cases to rather complete consideration in most cases. This consideration has been assured by many court decisions upholding the National Environmental Policy Act and the regulations of the Council on Environmental Quality. The CEQ regulations require the preparation of an environmental impact statement for any major federal action significantly affecting the quality of the human environment. The regulations also require substantial public involvement in the process. However, the requirements of NEPA are only procedural and are not substantive. Thus, NEPA is satisfied by the preparation of an adequate EIS, and the agency need not meet any requirements under NEPA other than the preparation of an adequate EIS. NEPA requires environmentally informed decisions, not necessarily environmentally correct decisions.

Nevertheless since 1970, the EIS process has focused public attention on the federal agencies' proposed projects, has forced these agencies to disclose the potential environmental impacts of their proposed projects, and has drawn public attention to environmental laws whose requirements are substantive and that apply to the project. Together, these have had the effect of forcing federal agencies to be more environmentally responsible in their activities.

Will NEPA and the EIS process survive long into the next millennium? Probably yes, although quite possibly in a different form. The emergence of the doctrine of functional equivalence may assure this. In any event, local environmental problems tend to become regional problems, regional problems tend to become national problems, and national problems tend to become global problems. As long as life exists on earth, some mechanism will be required to consider and solve these problems.

NATIONAL ENVIRONMENTAL POLICY ACT

42 U.S.C. 4321 et seq.

PURPOSE

42 USC 4321

Sec. 2. The purposes of this Act are: To declare a national policy which will encourage productive and enjoyable harmony between man and his environment; to promote efforts which will prevent or eliminate damage to the environment and biosphere and stimulate the health and welfare of man; to enrich the understanding of the ecological systems and natural resources important to the Nation; and to establish a Council on Environmental Quality.

TITLE I - POLICIES AND GOALS

CONGRESSIONAL DECLARATION OF NATIONAL ENVIRONMENTAL POLICY

42 USC 4331

Sec. 101. (a) The Congress, recognizing the profound impact of man's activity on the interrelations of all components of the natural environment, particularly the profound influences of population growth, high-density urbanization, industrial expansion, resource exploitation, and new and expanding technological advances and recognizing further the critical importance of restoring and maintaining environmental quality to the overall welfare and development of man, declares that it is the continuing policy of the Federal Government, in cooperation with State and local governments, and other concerned public and private organizations, to use all practicable means and measures, including financial and technical assistance, in a manner calculated to foster and promote the general welfare, to create and maintain conditions under which man and nature can exist in productive harmony, and fulfill the social, economic, and other requirements of present and future generations of Americans.

(b) In order to carry out the policy set forth in this Act, it is the continuing responsibility of the Federal Government to use all practicable means, consistent with other essential considerations of national policy to improve and coordinate Federal plans, functions, programs, and resources to the end that the Nation may--
(1) fulfill the responsibilities of each generation as trustee of the environment for succeeding generations;
(2) assure for all Americans safe, healthful, productive and esthetically and culturally pleasing surroundings;

(3) attain the widest range of beneficial uses of the environment without degradation, risk to health or safety, or other undesirable and unintended consequences;

(4) preserve important historic, cultural, and natural aspects of our national heritage, and maintain, wherever possible, an environment which supports diversity and variety of individual choice;

(5) achieve a balance between population and resource use which will permit high standards of living and a wide sharing of life's amenities; and

(6) enhance the quality of renewable resources and approach the maximum attainable recycling of depletable resources.

(c) The Congress recognizes that each person should enjoy a healthful environment and that each person has a responsibility to contribute to the preservation and enhancement of the environment.

COOPERATION OF AGENCIES; REPORTS; AVAILABILITY OF INFORMATION; RECOMMENDATIONS; INTERNATIONAL AND NATIONAL COORDINATION OF EFFORTS

42 USC 4332

Sec. 102. The Congress authorizes and directs that, to the fullest extent possible: (1) the policies, regulations, and public laws of the United States shall be interpreted and administered in accordance with the policies set forth in this Act, and (2) all agencies of the Federal Government shall--

(A) utilize a systematic, interdisciplinary approach which will insure the integrated use of the natural and social sciences and the environmental design arts in planning and in decisionmaking which may have an impact on man's environment;

(B) identify and develop methods and procedures, in consultation with the Council on Environmental Quality established by title II of this Act, which will insure that presently unquantified environmental amenities and values may be given appropriate consideration in decisionmaking along with economic and technical considerations;

(C) include in every recommendation or report on proposals for legislation and other major Federal actions significantly affecting the quality of the human environment, a detailed statement by the responsible official on--

(I) the environmental impact of the proposed action,

(ii) any adverse environmental effects which cannot be avoided should the proposal be implemented,

(iii) alternatives to the proposed action,

(iv) the relationship between local short-term uses of man's environment and the maintenance and enhancement of long-term productivity, and

(v) any irreversible and irretrievable commitments of resources which would be involved in the proposed action should it be implemented.

Prior to making any detailed statement, the responsible Federal official shall consult with and obtain the comments of any Federal agency which has jurisdiction by law or special expertise with respect to any environmental impact involved. Copies of such statement and the comments and views of the appropriate Federal, State, and local agencies, which are authorized to develop and enforce environmental standards, shall be made available to the President, the Council on Environmental Quality and to the public as provided by section 552 of title 5, United States Code, and shall accompany the proposal through the existing agency review process.

(D) Any detailed statement required under subparagraph (C) after January 1, 1970, for any major Federal action funded under a program of grants to States shall not be deemed to be legally insufficient solely by reason of having been prepared by a State agency or official, if:

(i) the State agency or official has statewide jurisdiction and has the responsibility for such action,

(ii) the responsible Federal official furnishes guidance and participates in such preparation,

(iii) the responsible Federal official independently evaluates such statement prior to its approval and adoption, and

(iv) after January 1, 1976 the responsible Federal official provides early notification to, and solicits the views of, any other State or any Federal land management entity of any action or any alternative thereto which may have significant impacts upon such State or affected Federal land management entity and, if there is any disagreement on such impacts, prepares a written assessment of such impacts and views for incorporation into such detailed statement.

The procedures in this subparagraph shall not relieve the Federal official of his responsibilities for the scope, objectivity, and content of the entire statement or of any other responsibility under this Act: and, further, this subparagraph does not affect the legal sufficiency of statements prepared by State agencies with less than statewide jurisdiction.

(E) study, develop, and describe appropriate alternatives to recommended courses of action in any proposal which involves unresolved conflicts concerning alternative uses of available resources;

(F) recognize the worldwide and long-range character of environmental problems and, where consistent with the foreign policy of the United States, lend appropriate support to initiatives, resolutions, and programs designed to maximize international cooperation in anticipating and preventing a decline in the quality of mankind's world environment;

(G) make available to States, counties, municipalities, institutions, and individuals, advice and information useful in restoring, maintaining, and enhancing the quality of the environment;

(H) initiate and utilize ecological information in the planning and development of resource-oriented projects; and

(I) assist the Council on Environmental Quality established by title II of this Act.

CONFORMITY OF ADMINISTRATIVE PROCEDURES TO
NATIONAL ENVIRONMENTAL POLICY

42 USC 4333

Sec. 103. All agencies of the Federal Government shall review their present statutory authority, administrative regulations, and current policies and procedures for the purpose of determining whether there are any deficiencies or inconsistencies therein which prohibit full compliance with the purposes and provisions of this Act and shall propose to the President not later than July 1, 1971, such measures as may be necessary to bring their authority and policies into conformity with the intent, purposes, and procedures set forth in this Act.

OTHER STATUTORY OBLIGATIONS OF AGENCIES

42 USC 4334

Sec. 104. Nothing in Section 102 or 103 shall in any way affect the specific statutory obligations of any Federal agency (1) to comply with criteria or standards of environmental quality, (2) to coordinate or consult with any other Federal or State agency, or (3) to act, or refrain from acting contingent upon the recommendations or certification of any other Federal or State agency.

EFFORTS SUPPLEMENTAL TO EXISTING AUTHORIZATIONS

42 USC 4335

Sec. 105. The policies and goals set forth in this Act are supplementary to those set forth in existing authorizations of Federal agencies.

TITLE II - COUNCIL ON ENVIRONMENTAL QUALITY

REPORTS TO CONGRESS;
RECOMMENDATIONS FOR LEGISLATION

42 USC 4341

Sec. 201. The President shall transmit to the Congress annually beginning July 1, 1970, an Environmental Quality Report (hereinafter referred to as the "report") which shall set forth (1) the status and condition of the major natural, manmade, or altered environmental classes of the Nation, including, but not limited to, the air, the aquatic, including marine, estuarine, and fresh water, and the terrestrial environment, including, but not limited to, the forest, dryland, wetland, range, urban, suburban, and rural environment; (2) current and foreseeable trends in the quality, management and utilization of such environments and the effects of those trends on the social, economic, and other requirements of the Nation; (3) the adequacy of available natural resources for fulfilling human and economic requirements of the Nation in the light of expected population pressures; (4) a review of the programs and activities (including regulatory activities) of the Federal Government, the State and local governments, and nongovernmental entities or individuals, with particular reference to their effect on the environment and on the conservation, development and utilization of natural resources; and (5) a program for remedying the deficiencies of existing programs and activities, together with recommendations for legislation.

ESTABLISHMENT; MEMBERSHIP; CHAIRMAN; APPOINTMENTS

42 USC 4342

Sec. 202. There is created in the Executive Office of the President a Council on Environmental Quality (hereinafter referred to as the "Council"). The Council shall be composed of three members who shall be appointed by the President to serve at his pleasure, by and with the advice and consent of the Senate. The President shall designate one of the members of the Council to serve as Chairman. Each member shall be a person who, as a result of his training, experience, and attainments, is exceptionally well qualified to analyze and interpret environmental trends and information of all kinds; to appraise programs and activities of the Federal Government in the light of the policy set forth in title I of this Act; to be conscious of and responsive to the scientific, economic, social, esthetic, and cultural needs and interests of the Nation; and to formulate and recommend national policies to promote the improvement of the quality of the environment.

EMPLOYMENT OF PERSONNEL, EXPERTS AND CONSULTANTS

42 USC 4343

Sec. 203. (a) The Council may employ such officers and employees as may be necessary to carry out its functions under this Act. In addition, the Council may employ and fix the compensation of such experts and consultants as may be necessary for the carrying out of its functions under this Act, in accordance with section 3109 of title 5, United States Code (but without regard to the last sentence thereof).

(b) Notwithstanding section 1342 of Title 31, the Council may accept and employ voluntary and uncompensated services in furtherance of the purposes of the Council.

DUTIES AND FUNCTIONS

42 USC 4344

Sec. 204. It shall be the duty and function of the Council--

(1) to assist and advise the President in the preparation of the Environmental Quality Report required by section 201;

(2) to gather timely and authoritative information concerning the conditions and trends in the quality of the environment both current and prospective, to analyze

and interpret such information for the purpose of determining whether such conditions and trends are interfering, or are likely to interfere, with the achievement of the policy set forth in title I of this Act, and to compile and submit to the President studies relating to such conditions and trends;

(3) to review and appraise the various programs and activities of the Federal Government in the light of the policy set forth in title I of this Act for the purpose of determining the extent to which such programs and activities are contributing to the achievement of such policy, and to make recommendations to the President with respect thereto;

(4) to develop and recommend to the President national policies to foster and promote the improvement of environmental quality to meet the conservation, social, economic, health, and other requirements and goals of the Nation;

(5) to conduct investigations, studies, surveys, research, and analyses relating to ecological systems and environmental quality;

(6) to document and define changes in the natural environment, including the plant and animal systems, and to accumulate necessary data and other information for a continuing analysis of these changes or trends and an interpretation of their underlying causes;

(7) to report at least once each year to the President on the state and condition of the environment; and

(8) to make and furnish such studies, reports thereon, and recommendations with respect to matters of policy and legislation as the President may request.

CONSULTATION WITH THE CITIZENS' ADVISORY COMMITTEE ON ENVIRONMENTAL QUALITY AND OTHER REPRESENTATIVES

42 USC 4345

Sec 205. In exercising its powers, functions, and duties under this Act, the Council shall—

(1) consult with the Citizens' Advisory Committee on Environmental Quality established by Executive Order numbered 11472, dated May 29, 1969, and with such representatives of science, industry, agriculture, labor, conservation, organizations, State and local governments and other groups, as it deems advisable; and

(2) utilize, to the fullest extent possible, the services, facilities, and information (including statistical information) of public and private agencies and organizations, and individuals, in order that duplication of effort and expense may be avoided, thus assuring that the Council's activities will not unnecessarily overlap or conflict with similar activities authorized by law and performed by established agencies.

TENURE AND COMPENSATION OF MEMBERS

42 USC 4346

Sec. 206. Members of the Council shall serve full time and the Chairman of the Council shall be compensated at the rate provided for Level II of the Executive Schedule Pay Rates (5 U.S.C. 5313). The other members of the Council shall be compensated at the rate provided for Level IV of the Executive Pay Rates (5 U.S.C. 5315).

TRAVEL REIMBURSEMENT BY PRIVATE ORGANIZATIONS AND FEDERAL, STATE, AND LOCAL GOVERNMENTS

42 USC 4346a

Sec. 207. The Council may accept reimbursements from any private nonprofit organization or from any department, agency, or instrumentality of the Federal Government, any State, or local government, for the reasonable travel expenses incurred by an officer or employee of the Council in connection with his attendance at any conference, seminar, or similar meeting conducted for the benefit of the Council.

EXPENDITURES IN SUPPORT OF INTERNATIONAL ACTIVITIES

42 USC 4346b

Sec. 208. The Council may make expenditures in support of its international activities, including expenditures for: (1) international travel; (2) activities in implementation of international agreements; and (3) the support of international exchange programs in the United States and in foreign countries.

AUTHORIZATION OF APPROPRIATIONS

42 USC 4347

Sec. 209. There are authorized to be appropriated to carry out the provisions of this Act not to exceed $300,000 for fiscal year 1970, $700,000 for fiscal year 1971, and $1,000,000 for each fiscal year thereafter.

PART 1500—PURPOSE, POLICY, AND MANDATE

Sec.
1500.1 Purpose.
1500.2 Policy.
1500.3 Mandate.
1500.4 Reducing paperwork.
1500.5 Reducing delay.
1500.6 Agency authority.

AUTHORITY: NEPA, the Environmental Quality Improvement Act of 1970, as amended (42 U.S.C. 4371 *et seq.*), sec. 309 of the Clean Air Act, as amended (42 U.S.C. 7609) and E.O. 11514, Mar. 5,1970, as amended by E.O. 11991, May 24, 1977).

SOURCE: 43 FR 55990, Nov. 28, 1978, unless otherwise noted.

§ 1500.1 Purpose.

(a) The National Environmental Policy Act (NEPA) is our basic national charter for protection of the environment. It establishes policy, sets goals (section 101), and provides means (section 102) for carrying out the policy. Section 102(2) contains "action-forcing" provisions to make sure that federal agencies act according to the letter and spirit of the Act. The regulations that follow implement section 102(2). Their purpose is to tell federal agencies what they must do to comply with the procedures and achieve the goals of the Act. The President, the federal agencies, and the courts share responsibility for enforcing the Act so as to achieve the substantive requirements of section 101.

(b) NEPA procedures must insure that environmental information is available to public officials and citizens before decisions are made and before actions are taken. The information must be of high quality. Accurate scientific analysis, expert agency comments, and public scrutiny are essential to implementing NEPA. Most important, NEPA documents must concentrate on the issues that are truly significant to the action in question, rather than amassing needless detail.

(c) Ultimately, of course, it is not better documents but better decisions that count. NEPA's purpose is not to generate paperwork—even excellent paperwork—but to foster excellent action. The NEPA process is intended to help public officials make decisions that are based on understanding of environmental consequences, and take actions that protect, restore, and enhance the environment. These regulations provide the direction to achieve this purpose.

§ 1500.2 Policy.

Federal agencies shall to the fullest extent possible:

(a) Interpret and administer the policies, regulations, and public laws of the United States in accordance with the policies set forth in the Act and in these regulations.

(b) Implement procedures to make the NEPA process more useful to decision makers and the public; to reduce paperwork and the accumulation of extraneous background data; and to emphasize real environmental issues and alternatives. Environmental impact statements shall be concise, clear, and to the point, and shall be supported by evidence that agencies have made the necessary environmental analyses.

(c) Integrate the requirements of NEPA with other planning and environmental review procedures required by law or by agency practice so that all such procedures run concurrently rather than consecutively.

(d) Encourage and facilitate public involvement in decisions which affect the quality of the human environment.

(e) Use the NEPA process to identify and assess the reasonable alternatives to proposed actions that will avoid or minimize adverse effects of these actions upon the quality of the human environment.

(f) Use all practicable means, consistent with the requirements of the Act and other essential considerations of national policy, to restore and enhance the quality of the human environment and avoid or minimize any possible adverse effects of their actions upon the quality of the human environment.

§ 1500.3 Mandate.

Parts 1500 through 1508 of this title provide regulations applicable to and binding on all Federal agencies for implementing the procedural provisions of the National Environmental Policy Act of 1969, as amended (Pub. L. 91-190, 42 U.S.C. 4321 *et seq.*) (NEPA or the Act) except where compliance would be inconsistent with other statutory requirements. These regulations are issued pursuant to NEPA, the Environmental Quality Improvement Act of 1970, as amended (42 U.S.C. 4371 *et seq.*) section 309 of the Clean Air Act, as amended (42 U.S.C. 7609) and Executive Order 11514, Protection and Enhancement of Environmental Quality (March 5, 1970, as amended by Executive Order 11991, May 24, 1977). These regulations, unlike the predecessor guidelines, are not confined to sec. 102(2)(C) (environmental impact statements). The regulations apply to the whole of section 102(2). The provisions of the Act and of these regulations must be read together as a whole in order to comply with the spirit and letter of the law. It is the Council's intention that judicial review of agency compliance with these regulations not occur before an agency has filed the final environmental impact statement, or has made a final finding of no significant impact (when such a finding will result in action affecting the environment), or takes action that will result in irreparable injury. Furthermore, it is the Council's intention that any trivial violation of these regulations not give rise to any independent cause of action.

§ 1500.4 Reducing paperwork.

Agencies shall reduce excessive paperwork by:

(a) Reducing the length of environmental impact statements (§1502.2(c)), by means such as setting appropriate page limits (§§ 1501.7(b)(1) and 1502.7).

(b) Preparing analytic rather than encyclopedic environmental impact statements (§ 1502.2(a)).

(c) Discussing only briefly issues other than significant ones (§1502.2(b)).

(d) Writing environmental impact statements in plain language (§ 1502.8).

(e) Following a clear format for environmental impact statements (§ 1502.10).

(f) Emphasizing the portions of the environmental impact statement that are useful to decision makers and the public (§§ 1502.14 and 1502.15) and reducing emphasis on background material (§ 1502.16).

(g) Using the scoping process, not only to identify significant environmental issues deserving of study, but also to deemphasize insignificant issues, narrowing the scope of the environmental impact statement process accordingly (§ 1501.7).

(h) Summarizing the environmental impact statement (§ 1502.12) and circulating the summary instead of the entire environmental impact statement if the latter is unusually long (§ 1502.19).

(i) Using program, policy, or plan environmental impact statements and tiering from statements of broad scope to those of narrower scope, to eliminate repetitive discussions of the same issues (§§ 1502.4 and 1502.20).

(j) Incorporating by reference (§ 1502.21).

(k) Integrating NEPA requirements with other environmental review and consultation requirements (§ 1502.25).

(l) Requiring comments to be as specific as possible (§ 1503.3).

(m) Attaching and circulating only changes to the draft environmental impact statement, rather than rewriting and circulating the entire statement when changes are minor (§ 1503.4(c)).

(n) Eliminating duplication with State and local procedures, by providing for joint preparation (§ 1506.2), and with other Federal procedures, by providing that an agency may adopt appropriate environmental documents prepared by another agency (§ 1506.3).

(o) Combining environmental documents with other documents (§ 1506.4).

(p) Using categorical exclusions to define categories of actions which do not individually or cumulatively have a significant effect on the human environment and which are therefore exempt from requirements to prepare an environmental impact statement (§ 1508.4).

(q) Using a finding of no significant impact when an action not otherwise excluded will not have a significant effect on the human environment and is therefore exempt from requirements to prepare an environmental impact statement (§ 1508.13).

[43 FR 55990, Nov. 29, 1978; 44 FR 873, Jan. 3, 1979]

§ 1500.5 Reducing delay.

Agencies shall reduce delay by:

(a) Integrating the NEPA process into early planning (§ 1501.2).

(b) Emphasizing interagency cooperation before the environmental impact statement is prepared, rather than submission of adversary comments on a completed document (§ 1501.6).

(c) Insuring the swift and fair resolution of lead agency disputes (§ 1501.5).

(d) Using the scoping process for an early identification of what are and what are not the real issues (§ 1501.7).

(e) Establishing appropriate time limits for the environmental impact statement process (§§ 1501.7(b)(2) and 1501.8).

(f) Preparing environmental impact statements early in the process (§ 1502.5).

(g) Integrating NEPA requirements with other environmental review and consultation requirements (§ 1502.25).

(h) Eliminating duplication with State and local procedures by providing for joint preparation (§ 1506.2) and with other Federal procedures by providing that an agency may adopt appropriate environmental documents prepared by another agency (§ 1506.3).

(i) Combining environmental documents with other documents (§ 1506.4).

(j) Using accelerated procedures for proposals for legislation (§ 1506.8).

(k) Using categorical exclusions to define categories of actions which do not individually or cumulatively have a significant effect on the human environment (§ 1508.4) and which are therefore exempt from requirements to prepare an environmental impact statement.

(l) Using a finding of no significant impact when an action not otherwise excluded will not have a significant effect on the human environment (§ 1508.13) and is therefore exempt from requirements to prepare an environmental impact statement.

§ 1500.6 Agency authority.

Each agency shall interpret the provisions of the Act as a supplement to its existing authority and as a mandate to view traditional policies and missions in the light of the Act's national environmental objectives. Agencies shall review their policies, procedures, and regulations accordingly and revise them as necessary to insure full compliance with the purposes and provisions of the Act. The phrase "to the fullest extent possible" in section 102 means that each agency of the Federal Government shall comply with that section unless existing law applicable to the agency's operations expressly prohibits or makes compliance impossible.

PART 1501—NEPA AND AGENCY PLANNING

Sec.
1501.1 Purpose.
1501.2 Apply NEPA early in the process.
1501.3 When to prepare an environmental assessment.
1501.4 Whether to prepare an environmental impact statement.
1501.5 Lead agencies.
1501.6 Cooperating agencies.
1501.7 Scoping.
1501.8 Time limits.

AUTHORITY: NEPA, the Environmental Quality Improvement Act of 1970, as amended (42 U.S.C. 4371 *et seq.*), sec. 309 of the Clean Air Act, as amended (42 U.S.C. 7609, and E.O. 11514 (Mar. 5, 1970, as amended by E.O. 11991, May 24, 1977).

SOURCE: 43 FR 55992, Nov. 29, 1978, unless otherwise noted.

§ 1501.1 Purpose.

The purposes of this part include:

(a) Integrating the NEPA process into early planning to insure appropriate consideration of NEPA's policies and to eliminate delay.

(b) Emphasizing cooperative consultation among agencies before the environmental impact statement is prepared rather than submission of adversary comments on a completed document.

(c) Providing for the swift and fair resolution of lead agency disputes.

(d) Identifying at an early stage the significant environmental issues deserving of study and deemphasizing insignificant issues, narrowing the scope of the environmental impact statement accordingly.

(e) Providing a mechanism for putting appropriate time limits on the environmental impact statement process.

§ 1501.2 Apply NEPA early in the process.

Agencies shall integrate the NEPA process with other planning at the earliest possible time to insure that planning and decisions reflect environmental values, to avoid delays later in the process, and to head off potential conflicts. Each agency shall:

(a) Comply with the mandate of section 102(2)(A) to "utilize a systematic, interdisciplinary approach which will insure the integrated use of the natural and social sciences and the environmental design arts in planning and in decisionmaking which may have an impact on man's environment," as specified by § 1507.2.

(b) Identify environmental effects and values in adequate detail so they can be compared to economic and technical analyses. Environmental documents and appropriate analyses shall be circulated and reviewed at the same time as other planning documents.

(c) Study, develop, and describe appropriate alternatives to recommended courses of action in any proposal which involves unresolved conflicts concerning alternative uses of available resources as provided by section 102(2)(E) of the Act.

(d) Provide for cases where actions are planned by private applicants or other non-Federal entities before Federal involvement so that:

(1) Policies or designated staff are available to advise potential applicants of studies or other information foreseeably required for later Federal action.

(2) The Federal agency consults early with appropriate State and local agencies and Indian tribes and with interested private persons and organizations when its own involvement is reasonably foreseeable.

(3) The Federal agency commences its NEPA process at the earliest possible time.

§ 1501.3 When to prepare an environmental assessment.

(a) Agencies shall prepare an environmental assessment (§ 1508.9) when necessary under the procedures adopted by individual agencies to supplement these regulations as described in § 1507.3. An assessment is not necessary if the agency has decided to prepare an environmental impact statement.

(b) Agencies may prepare an environmental assessment on any action at any time in order to assist agency planning and decisionmaking.

§ 1501.4 Whether to prepare an environmental impact statement.

In determining whether to prepare an environmental impact statement the Federal agency shall:

(a) Determine under its procedures supplementing these regulations (described in § 1507.3) whether the proposal is one which:

(1) Normally requires an environmental impact statement, or

(2) Normally does not require either an environmental impact statement or an environmental assessment (categorical exclusion).

(b) If the proposed action is not covered by paragraph (a) of this section, prepare an environmental assessment (§ 1508.9). The agency shall involve environmental agencies, applicants, and the public, to the extent practicable, in preparing assessments required by § 1508.9(a)(1).

(c) Based on the environmental assessment make its determination whether to prepare an environmental impact statement.

(d) Commence the scoping process (§ 1501.7), if the agency will prepare an environmental impact statement.

(e) Prepare a finding of no significant impact (§ 1508.13), if the agency determines on the basis of the environmental assessment not to prepare a statement.

(1) The agency shall make the finding of no significant impact available to the affected public as specified in § 1506.6.

(2) In certain limited circumstances, which the agency may cover in its procedures under § 1507.3, the agency shall make the finding of no significant impact available for public review (including State and areawide clearinghouses) for 30 days before the agency makes its final determination whether to prepare an environmental impact statement and before the action may begin. The circumstances are:

(i) The proposed action is, or is closely similar to, one which normally requires the preparation of an environmental impact statement under the procedures adopted by the agency pursuant to § 1507.3, or

(ii) The nature of the proposed action is one without precedent.

§ 1501.5 Lead agencies.

(a) A lead agency shall supervise the preparation of an environmental impact statement if more than one Federal agency either:

(1) Proposes or is involved in the same action; or

(2) Is involved in a group of actions directly related to each other because of their functional interdependence or geographical proximity.

(b) Federal, State, or local agencies including at least one Federal agency may act as joint lead agencies to prepare an environmental impact statement (§ 1506.2).

(c) If an action falls within the provisions of paragraph (a) of this section the potential lead agencies shall determine by letter or memorandum which agency shall be the lead agency and which shall be cooperating agencies. The agencies shall resolve the lead agency question so as not to cause delay. If there is disagreement among the agencies, the following factors (which are listed in order of descending importance) shall determine lead agency designation:

(1) Magnitude of agency's involvement.

(2) Project approval/disapproval authority.

(3) Expertise concerning the action's environmental effects.

(4) Duration of agency's involvement.

(5) Sequence of agency's involvement.

(d) Any Federal agency, or any State or local agency or private person substantially affected by the absence of lead agency designation, may make a written request to the potential lead agencies that a lead agency be designated.

(e) If Federal agencies are unable to agree on which agency will be the lead agency or if the procedure described in paragraph (c) of this section has not resulted within 45 days in a lead agency designation, any of the agencies or persons concerned may file a request with the Council asking it to determine which Federal agency shall be the lead agency.

A copy of the request shall be transmitted to each potential lead agency. The request shall consist of:

(1) A precise description of the nature and extent of the proposed action.

(2) A detailed statement of why each potential lead agency should or should not be the lead agency under the criteria specified in paragraph (c) of this section.

(f) A response may be filed by any potential lead agency concerned within 20 days after a request is filed with the Council. The Council shall determine as soon as possible but not later than 20 days after receiving the request and all responses to it which Federal agency shall be the lead agency and which other Federal agencies shall be cooperating agencies.

[43 FR 55992, Nov. 29, 1978; 44 FR 873, Jan. 3, 1979]

§ 1501.6 Cooperating agencies.

The purpose of this section is to emphasize agency cooperation early in the NEPA process. Upon request of the lead agency, any other Federal agency which has jurisdiction by law shall be a cooperating agency. In addition any other Federal agency which has special expertise with respect to any environmental issue, which should be addressed in the statement may be a cooperating agency upon request of the lead agency. An agency may request the lead agency to designate it a cooperating agency.

(a) The lead agency shall:

(1) Request the participation of each cooperating agency in the NEPA process at the earliest possible time.

(2) Use the environmental analysis and proposals of cooperating agencies with jurisdiction by law or special expertise, to the maximum extent possible consistent with its responsibility as lead agency.

(3) Meet with a cooperating agency at the latter's request.

(b) Each cooperating agency shall:

(1) Participate in the NEPA process at the earliest possible time.

(2) Participate in the scoping process (described below in § 1501.7).

(3) Assume on request of the lead agency responsibility for developing information and preparing environmental analyses including portions of the environmental impact statement concerning which the cooperating agency has special expertise.

(4) Make available staff support at the lead agency's request to enhance the latter's interdisciplinary capability.

(5) Normally use its own funds. The lead agency shall, to the extent available funds permit, fund those major activities or analyses it requests from cooperating agencies. Potential lead agencies shall include such funding requirements in their budget requests.

(c) A cooperating agency may in response to a lead agency's request for assistance in preparing the environmental impact statement (described in paragraph (b)(3), (4), or (5) of this section) reply that other program commitments preclude any involvement or the degree of involvement requested in the action that is the subject of the environmental impact statement. A copy of this reply shall be submitted to the Council.

§ 1501.7 Scoping.

There shall be an early and open process for determining the scope of issues to be addressed and for identifying the significant issues related to a proposed action. This process shall be termed scoping. As soon as practicable after its decision to prepare an environmental impact statement and before the scoping process the lead agency shall publish a notice of intent (§ 1508.22) in the *FEDERAL REGISTER* except as provided in § 1507.3(e).

(a) As part of the scoping process the lead agency shall:

(1) Invite the participation of affected Federal, State, and local agencies, any affected Indian tribe, the proponent of the action, and other interested persons (including those who might not be in accord with the action on environmental grounds), unless there is a limited exception under § 1507.3(c). An agency may give notice in accordance with § 1506.6.

(2) Determine the scope (§ 1508.25) and the significant issues to be analyzed in depth in the environmental impact statement.

(3) Identify and eliminate from detailed study the issues which are not significant or which have been covered by prior environmental review (§ 1506.3), narrowing the discussion of these issues in the statement to a brief presentation of why they will not have a significant effect on the human environment or providing a reference to their coverage elsewhere.

(4) Allocate assignments for preparation of the environmental impact statement among the lead and cooperating agencies, with the lead agency retaining responsibility for the statement.

(5) Indicate any public environmental assessments and other environmental impact statements which are being or will be prepared that are related to but are not part of the scope of the impact statement under consideration.

(6) Identify other environmental review and consultation requirements so the lead and cooperating agencies may prepare other required analyses and studies concurrently with, and integrated with, the environmental impact statement as provided in § 1502.25.

(7) Indicate the relationship between the timing of the preparation of environmental analyses and the agency's tentative planning and decisionmaking schedule.

(b) As part of the scoping process the lead agency may:

(1) Set page limits on environmental documents (§ 1502.7).

(2) Set time limits (§ 1501.8).

(3) Adopt procedures under § 1507.3 to combine its environmental assessment process with its scoping process.

(4) Hold an early scoping meeting or meetings which may be integrated with any other early planning meeting the agency has. Such a scoping meeting will often be appropriate when the impacts of a particular action are confined to specific sites.

(c) An agency shall revise the determinations made under paragraphs (a) and (b) of this section if substantial changes are made later in the proposed action, or if significant new circumstances or information arise which bear on the proposal or its impacts.

§ 1501.8 Time limits.

Although the Council has decided that prescribed universal time limits for the entire NEPA process are too inflexible, Federal agencies are encouraged to set time limits appropriate to individual actions (consistent with the time intervals required by § 1506.10). When multiple agencies are involved the reference to agency below means lead agency.

(a) The agency shall set time limits if an applicant for the proposed action requests them: *Provided,* That the limits are consistent with the purposes of NEPA and other essential considerations of national policy.

(b) The agency may:

(1) Consider the following factors in determining time limits:

(i) Potential for environmental harm.

(ii) Size of the proposed action.

(iii) State of the art of analytic techniques.

(iv) Degree of public need for the proposed action, including the consequences of delay.

(v) Number of persons and agencies affected.

(vi) Degree to which relevant information is known and if not known the time required for obtaining it.

(vii) Degree to which the action is controversial.

(viii) Other time limits imposed on the agency by law, regulations, or executive order.

(2) Set overall time limits or limits for each constituent part of the NEPA process, which may include:

(i) Decision on whether to prepare an environmental impact statement (if not already decided).

(ii) Determination of the scope of the environmental impact statement.

(iii) Preparation of the draft environmental impact statement.

(iv) Review of any comments on the draft environmental impact statement from the public and agencies.

(v) Preparation of the final environmental impact statement.

(vi) Review of any comments on the final environmental impact statement.

(vii) Decision on the action based in part on the environmental impact statement.

(3) Designate a person (such as the project manager or a person in the agency's office with NEPA responsibilities) to expedite the NEPA process.

(c) State or local agencies or members of the public may request a Federal Agency to set time limits.

PART 1502—ENVIRONMENTAL IMPACT STATEMENT

AUTHORITY: NEPA, the Environmental Quality Improvement Act of 1970, as amended (42 U.S.C. 4371 *et seq.*), sec. 309 of the Clean Air Act, as amended (42 U.S.C. 7609), and E.O. 11514 (Mar. 5,1970, as amended by E.O. 11991 May 24, 1977).

SOURCE: 43 FR 55994, Nov. 29, 1978, unless otherwise noted.

§ 1502.1 Purpose.

The primary purpose of an environmental impact statement is to serve as an action-forcing device to insure that the policies and goals defined in the Act are infused into the ongoing programs and actions of the Federal Government. It shall provide full and fair discussion of significant environmental impacts and shall inform decision makers and the public of the reasonable alternatives which would avoid or minimize adverse impacts or enhance the quality of the human environment. Agencies shall focus on significant environmental issues and alternatives and shall reduce paperwork and the accumulation of extraneous background data. Statements shall be concise, clear, and to the point, and shall be supported by evidence that the agency has made the necessary environmental analyses. An environmental impact statement is more than a disclosure document. It shall be used by Federal officials in conjunction with other relevant material to plan actions and make decisions.

§ 1502.2 Implementation.

To achieve the purposes set forth in § 1502.1 agencies shall prepare environmental impact statements in the following manner:

(a) Environmental impact statements shall be analytic rather than encyclopedic.

(b) Impacts shall be discussed in proportion to their significance. There shall be only brief discussion of other than significant issues. As in a finding of no significant impact, there should be only enough discussion to show why more study is not warranted.

(c) Environmental impact statements shall be kept concise and shall be no longer than absolutely necessary to comply with NEPA and with these regulations. Length should vary first with potential environmental problems and then with project size.

(d) Environmental impact statements shall state how alternatives considered in it and decisions based on it will or will not achieve the requirements of sections 101 and 102(1) of the Act and other environmental laws and policies.

(e) The range of alternatives discussed in environmental impact statements shall encompass those to be considered by the ultimate agency decision maker.

(f) Agencies shall not commit resources prejudicing selection of alternatives before making a final decision (§ 1506.1).

(g) Environmental impact statements shall serve as the means of assessing the environmental impact of proposed agency actions, rather than justifying decisions already made.

§ 1502.3 Statutory requirements for statements.

As required by sec. 102(2)(C) of NEPA environmental impact statements (§ 1508.11) are to be included in every recommendation or report.

On proposals (§ 1508.23).

For legislation and (§ 1508.17).

Other major Federal actions (§ 1508.18).

Significantly (§ 1508.27).

Affecting (§§ 1508.3, 1508.8).

The quality of the human environment (§ 1508.14).

§ 1502.4 Major Federal actions requiring the preparation of environmental impact statements.

(a) Agencies shall make sure the proposal which is the subject of an environmental impact statement is properly defined. Agencies shall use the criteria for scope (§ 1508.25) to determine which proposal(s) shall be the subject of a particular statement. Proposals or parts of proposals which are related to each other closely enough to be, in effect, a single course of action shall be evaluated in a single impact statement.

(b) Environmental impact statements may be prepared, and are sometimes required, for broad Federal actions such as the adoption of new agency programs or regulations (§ 1508.18). Agencies shall prepare statements on broad actions so that they are relevant to policy and are timed to coincide with meaningful points in agency planning and decisionmaking.

(c) When preparing statements on broad actions (including proposals by more than one agency), agencies may find it useful to evaluate the proposal(s) in one of the following ways:

(1) Geographically, including actions occurring in the same general location, such as body of water, region, or metropolitan area.

(2) Generically, including actions which have relevant similarities, such as common timing, impacts, alternatives, methods of implementation, media, or subject matter.

(3) By stage of technological development including federal or federally assisted research, development or demonstration programs for new technologies which, if applied, could significantly affect the quality of the human environment. Statements shall be prepared on such programs and shall be available before the program has reached a stage of investment or commitment to implementation likely to determine subsequent development or restrict later alternatives.

(d) Agencies shall as appropriate employ scoping (§ 1501.7), tiering (§ 1502.20), and other methods listed in §§ 1500.4 and 1500.5 to relate broad and narrow actions and to avoid duplication and delay.

§1502.5 Timing.

An agency shall commence preparation of an environmental impact statement as close as possible to the time the agency is developing or is presented with a proposal (§ 1508.23) so that preparation can be completed in time for the final statement to be included in any recommendation or report on the proposal. The statement shall be prepared early enough so that it can serve practically as an important contribution to the decisionmaking process and will not be used to rationalize or justify decisions already made (§§ 1500.2(c), 1501.2, and 1502.2). For instance:

(a) For projects directly undertaken by Federal agencies the environmental impact statement shall be prepared at the feasibility analysis (go-no go) stage and may be supplemented at a later stage if necessary.

(b) For applications to the agency appropriate environmental assessments or statements shall be commenced no later than immediately after the application is received. Federal agencies are encouraged to begin preparation of such assessments or statements earlier, preferably jointly with applicable State or local agencies.

(c) For adjudication, the final environmental impact statement shall normally precede the final staff recommendation and that portion of the public hearing related to the impact study. In appropriate circumstances the statement may follow preliminary hearings designed to gather information for use in the statements.

(d) For informal rulemaking the draft environmental impact statement shall normally accompany the proposed rule.

§ 1502.6 Interdisciplinary preparation.

Environmental impact statements shall be prepared using an interdisciplinary approach which will insure the integrated use of the natural and social sciences and the environmental design arts (section 102(2)(A) of the Act). The disciplines of the preparers shall be appropriate to the scope and issues identified in the scoping process (§ 1501.7).

§ 1502.7 Page limits.

The text of final environmental impact statements (e.g., paragraphs (d) through (g) of § 1502.10) shall normally be less than 150 pages and for proposals of unusual scope or complexity shall normally be less than 300 pages.

§ 1502.8 Writing.

Environmental impact statements shall be written in plain language and may use appropriate graphics so that decision makers and the public can readily understand them. Agencies should employ writers of clear prose or editors to write, review, or edit statements, which will be based upon the analysis and supporting data from the natural and social sciences and the environmental design arts.

§ 1502.9 Draft, final, and supplemental statements.

Except for proposals for legislation as provided in § 1506.8 environmental impact statements shall be prepared in two stages and may be supplemented.

(a) Draft environmental impact statements shall be prepared in accordance with the scope decided upon in the scoping process. The lead agency shall work with the cooperating agencies and shall obtain comments as required in part 1503 of this chapter. The draft statement must fulfill and satisfy to the fullest extent possible the requirements established for final statements in section 102(2)(C) of the Act. If a draft statement is so inadequate as to preclude meaningful analysis, the agency shall prepare and circulate a revised draft of the appropriate portion. The agency shall make every effort to disclose and discuss at appropriate points in the draft statement all major points of view on the environmental impacts of the alternatives including the proposed action.

(b) Final environmental impact statements shall respond to comments as required in part 1503 of this chapter. The agency shall discuss at appropriate points in the final statement any responsible opposing view which was not adequately discussed in the draft statement and shall indicate the agency's response to the issues raised.

(c) Agencies:

(1) Shall prepare supplements to either draft or final environmental impact statements if:

(i) The agency makes substantial changes in the proposed action that are relevant to environmental concerns; or

(ii) There are significant new circumstances or information relevant to environmental concerns and bearing on the proposed action or its impacts.

(2) May also prepare supplements when the agency determines that the purposes of the Act will be furthered by doing so.

(3) Shall adopt procedures for introducing a supplement into its formal administrative record, if such a record exists.

(4) Shall prepare, circulate, and file a supplement to a statement in the same fashion (exclusive of scoping) as a draft and final statement unless alternative procedures are approved by the Council.

§ 1502.10 Recommended format.

Agencies shall use a format for environmental impact statements which will encourage good analysis and clear presentation of the alternatives including the proposed action. The following standard format for environmental impact statements should be followed unless the agency determines that there is a compelling reason to do otherwise:

(a) Cover sheet.

(b) Summary.

(c) Table of contents.

(d) Purpose of and need for action.

(e) Alternatives including proposed action (sections 102(2)(C)(iii) and 102(2)(E) of the Act).

(f) Affected environment.

(g) Environmental consequences (especially sections 102(2)(C)(i), (ii), (iv), and (v) of the Act).

(h) List of preparers.

(i) List of Agencies, Organizations, and persons to whom copies of the statement are sent.

(j) Index.

(k) Appendices (if, any).

If a different format is used, it shall include paragraphs (a), (b), (c), (h), (i), and (j), of this section and shall include the substance of paragraphs (d), (e), (f), (g), and (k) of this section, as further described in §§ 1502.11 through 1502.18, in any appropriate format.

§ 1502.11 Cover sheet.

The cover sheet shall not exceed one page. It shall include:

(a) A list of the responsible agencies including the lead agency and any cooperating agencies.

(b) The title of the proposed action that is the subject of the statement (and if appropriate the titles of related cooperating agency actions), together with the State(s) and county(ies) (or other jurisdiction if applicable) where the action is located.

(c) The name, address, and telephone number of the person at the agency who can supply further information.

(d) A designation of the statement as a draft, final, or draft or final supplement.

(e) A one paragraph abstract of the statement.

(f) The date by which comments must be received (computed in cooperation with EPA under § 1506.10).

The information required by this section may be entered on Standard Form 424 (in items 4, 6, 7,10, and 18).

§ 1502.12 Summary.

Each environmental impact statement shall contain a summary which adequately and accurately summarizes the statement. The summary shall stress the major conclusions, areas of controversy (including issues raised by agencies and the public), and the issues to be resolved (including the choice among alternatives). The summary will normally not exceed 15 pages.

§1502.13 Purpose and need.

The statement shall briefly specify the underlying purpose and need to which the agency is responding in proposing the alternatives including the proposed action.

§ 1502.14 Alternatives including the proposed action.

This section is the heart of the environmental impact statement. Based on the information and analysis presented in the sections on the Affected Environment (§ 1502.15) and the Environmental Consequences (§ 1502.16), it should present the environmental impacts of the proposal and the alternatives in comparative form, thus sharply defining the issues and providing a clear basis for choice among options by the decisionmaker and the public. In this section agencies shall:

(a) Rigorously explore and objectively evaluate all reasonable alternatives, and for alternatives which were eliminated from detailed study, briefly discuss the reasons for their having been eliminated.

(b) Devote substantial treatment to each alternative considered in detail including the proposed action so that reviewers may evaluate their comparative merits.

(c) Include reasonable alternatives not within the jurisdiction of the lead agency.

(d) Include the alternative of no action.

(e) Identify the agency's preferred alternative or alternatives, if one or more exists, in the draft statement and identify such alternative in the final statement unless another law prohibits the expression of such a preference.

(f) Include appropriate mitigation measures not already included in the proposed action or alternatives.

§ 1502.15 Affected environment.

The environmental impact statement shall succinctly describe the environment of the area(s) to be affected or created by the alternatives under consideration. The descriptions shall be no longer than is necessary to understand the effects of the alternatives. Data and analyses in a statement shall be commensurate with the importance of the impact, with less important material summarized, consolidated, or simply referenced. Agencies shall avoid useless bulk in statements and shall concentrate effort and attention on important issues. Verbose descriptions of the affected environment are themselves no measure of the adequacy of an environmental impact statement.

§ 1502.16 Environmental consequences.

This section forms the scientific and analytic basis for the comparisons under § 1502.14. It shall consolidate the discussions of those elements required by sections 102(2)(C)(i), (ii), (iv), and (v) of NEPA which are within the scope of the statement and as much of section 102(2)(C)(iii) as is necessary to support the comparisons. The discussion will include the environmental impacts of the alternatives including the proposed action, any adverse environmental effects which cannot be avoided should the proposal be implemented, the relationship between short-term uses of man's environment and the maintenance and enhancement of long-term productivity, and any irreversible or irretrievable commitments of resources which would be involved in the proposal should it be implemented. This section should not duplicate discussions in § 1502.14. It shall include discussions of:

(a) Direct effects and their significance (§ 1508.8).

(b) Indirect effects and their significance (§ 1508.8).

(c) Possible conflicts between the proposed action and the objectives of Federal, regional, State, and local (and in the case of a reservation, Indian tribe) land use plans, policies and controls for the area concerned. (See § 1506.2(d).)

(d) The environmental effects of alternatives including the proposed action. The comparisons under § 1502.14 will be based on this discussion.

(e) Energy requirements and conservation potential of various alternatives and mitigation measures.

(f) Natural or depletable resource requirements and conservation potential of various alternatives and mitigation measures.

(g) Urban quality, historic and cultural resources, and the design of the built environment, including the reuse and conservation potential of various alternatives and mitigation measures.

(h) Means to mitigate adverse environmental impacts (if not fully covered under § 1502.14(f)).

[43 FR 55994, Nov. 29, 1978; 44 FR 873, Jan. 3, 1979]

§ 1502.17 List of preparers.

The environmental impact statement shall list the names, together with their qualifications (expertise, experience, professional disciplines), of the persons who were primarily responsible for preparing the environmental impact statement or significant background papers, including basic components of the statement (§§ 1502.6 and 1502.8). Where possible the persons who are responsible for a particular analysis, including analyses in background papers, shall be identified. Normally the list will not exceed two pages.

§ 1502.18 Appendix.

If an agency prepares an appendix to an environmental impact statement the appendix shall:

(a) Consist of material prepared in connection with an environmental impact statement (as distinct from material which is not so prepared and which is incorporated by reference (§ 1502.21)).

(b) Normally consist of material which substantiates any analysis fundamental to the impact statement.

(c) Normally be analytic and relevant to the decision to be made.

(d) Be circulated with the environmental impact statement or be readily available on request.

§ 1502.19 Circulation of the environmental impact statement.

Agencies shall circulate the entire draft and final environmental impact statements except for certain appendices as provided in § 1502.18(d) and unchanged statements as provided in § 1503.4(c). However, if the statement is unusually long, the agency may circulate the summary instead, except that the entire statement shall be furnished to:

(a) Any Federal agency which has jurisdiction by law or special expertise with respect to any environmental impact involved and any appropriate Federal, State or local agency authorized to develop and enforce environmental standards.

(b) The applicant, if any.

(c) Any person, organization, or agency requesting the entire environmental impact statement.

(d) In the case of a final environmental impact statement any person, organization, or agency which submitted substantive comments on the draft.

If the agency circulates the summary and thereafter receives a timely request for the entire statement and for additional time to comment, the time for that requester only shall be extended by at least 15 days beyond the minimum period.

§ 1502.20 Tiering.

Agencies are encouraged to tier their environmental impact statements to eliminate repetitive discussions of the same issues and to focus on the actual issues ripe for decision at each level of environmental review (§ 1508.28). Whenever a broad environmental impact statement has been prepared (such as a program or policy statement) and a subsequent statement or environmental assessment is then prepared on an action included within the entire program or policy (such as a site specific action) the subsequent statement or environmental assessment need only summarize the issues discussed in the broader statement and incorporate discussions from the broader statement by reference and shall concentrate on the issues specific to the subsequent action. The subsequent document shall state where the earlier document is available. Tiering may also be appropriate for different stages of actions. (Section 1508.28).

§ 1502.21 Incorporation by reference.

Agencies shall incorporate material into an environmental impact statement by reference when the effect will be to cut down on bulk without impeding agency and public review of the action. The incorporated material shall be cited in the statement and its content briefly described. No material may be incorporated by reference unless it is reasonably available for inspection by potentially interested persons within the time allowed for comment. Material based on proprietary data which is itself not available for review and comment shall not be incorporated by reference.

§ 1502.22 Incomplete or unavailable information.

When an agency is evaluating reasonably foreseeable significant adverse effects on the human environment in an environmental impact statement and there is incomplete or unavailable information, the agency shall always make clear that such information is lacking.

(a) If the incomplete information relevant to reasonably foreseeable significant adverse impacts is essential to a reasoned choice among alternatives and the overall costs of obtaining it are not exorbitant, the agency shall include the information in the environmental impact statement.

(b) If the information relevant to reasonably foreseeable significant adverse impacts cannot be obtained because the overall costs of obtaining it are exorbitant or the means to obtain it are not known, the agency shall include within the environmental impact statement:

(1) A statement that such information is incomplete or unavailable; (2) a statement of the relevance of the incomplete or unavailable information to evaluating reasonably foreseeable significant adverse impacts on the human environment; (3) a summary of existing credible scientific evidence which is relevant to evaluating the reasonably foreseeable significant adverse impacts on the human environment, and (4) the agency's evaluation of such impacts based upon theoretical approaches or research methods generally accepted in the scientific community. For the purposes of this section, "reasonably foreseeable" includes impacts which have catastrophic consequences, even if their probability of occurrence is low, provided that the analysis of the impacts is supported by credible scientific evidence, is not based on pure conjecture, and is within the rule of reason.

(c) The amended regulation will be applicable to all environmental impact statements for which a Notice of Intent (40 CFR 1508.22) is published in the FEDERAL REGISTER on or after May 27, 1986. For environmental impact statements in progress, agencies may choose to comply with the requirements of either the original or amended regulation.

[51 FR 15625, Apr. 25, 1986]

§ 1502.23 Cost benefit analysis.

If a cost-benefit analysis relevant to the choice among environmentally different alternatives is being considered for the proposed action, it shall be incorporated by reference or appended to the statement as an aid in evaluating the environmental consequences. To assess the adequacy of compliance with section 102(2)(B) of the Act the statement shall, when a cost-benefit analysis is prepared, discuss the relationship between that analysis and any analyses of unquantified environmental impacts, values, and amenities. For purposes of complying with the Act, the weighing of the merits and drawbacks of the various alternatives need not be displayed in a monetary cost-benefit analysis and should not be when there are important qualitative considerations. In any event, an environmental impact statement should at least indicate those considerations, including factors not related to environmental quality, which are likely to be relevant and important to a decision.

§ 1502.24 Methodology and scientific accuracy.

Agencies shall insure the professional integrity, including scientific integrity, of the discussions and analyses in environmental impact statements. They shall identify any methodologies used and shall make explicit reference by footnote to the scientific and other sources relied upon for conclusions in the statement. An agency may place discussion of methodology in an appendix.

§ 1502.25 Environmental review and consultation requirements.

(a) To the fullest extent possible, agencies shall prepare draft environmental impact statements concurrently with and integrated with environmental impact analyses and related surveys and studies required by the Fish and Wildlife Coordination Act (16 U.S.C. 661 *et seq.*), the National Historic Preservation Act of 1966 (16 U.S.C. 470 *et seq.*), the Endangered Species Act of 1973 (16 U.S.C. 1531 *et seq.*), and other environmental review laws and executive orders.

(b) The draft environmental impact statement shall list all Federal permits, licenses, and other entitlements which must be obtained in implementing the proposal. If it is uncertain whether a Federal permit, license, or other entitlement is necessary, the draft environmental impact statement shall so indicate.

PART 1503—COMMENTING

AUTHORITY: NEPA, the Environmental Quality Improvement Act of 1970, as amended (42 U.S.C. 4371 *et seq.*), sec. 309 of the Clean Air Act, as amended (42 U.S.C. 7609), and E.O. 11514 (Mar. 5, 1970, as amended by E.O. 11991, May 24, 1977).

SOURCE: 43 FR 55997, Nov. 29, 1978, unless otherwise noted.

§ 1503.1 Inviting comments.

(a) After preparing a draft environmental impact statement and before preparing a final environmental impact statement the agency shall:

(1) Obtain the comments of any Federal agency which has jurisdiction by law or special expertise with respect to any environmental impact involved or which is authorized to develop and enforce environmental standards.

(2) Request the comments of:

(i) Appropriate State and local agencies which are authorized to develop and enforce environmental standards;

(ii) Indian tribes, when the effects may be on a reservation; and

(iii) Any agency which has requested that it receive statements on actions of the kind proposed.

Office of Management and Budget Circular A-95 (Revised), through its system of clearinghouses, provides a means of securing the views of State and local environmental agencies. The clearinghouses may be used, by mutual agreement of the lead agency and the clearinghouse, for securing State and local reviews of the draft environmental impact statements.

(3) Request comments from the applicant, if any.

(4) Request comments from the public, affirmatively soliciting comments from those persons or organizations who may be interested or affected.

(b) An agency may request comments on a final environmental impact statement before the decision is finally made. In any case other agencies or persons may make comments before the final decision unless a different time is provided under § 1506.10.

§ 1503.2 Duty to comment.

Federal agencies with jurisdiction by law or special expertise with respect to any environmental impact involved and agencies which are authorized to develop and enforce environmental standards shall comment on statements within their jurisdiction, expertise, or authority. Agencies shall comment within the time period specified for comment in § 1506.10. A Federal agency may reply that it has no comment. If a cooperating agency is satisfied that its views are adequately reflected in the environmental impact statement, it should reply that it has no comment.

§ 1503.3 Specificity of comment.

(a) Comments on an environmental impact statement or on a proposed action shall be as specific as possible and may address either the adequacy of the statement or the merits of the alternatives discussed or both.

(b) When a commenting agency criticizes a lead agency's predictive methodology, the commenting agency should describe the alternative methodology which it prefers and why.

(c) A cooperating agency shall specify in its comments whether it needs additional information to fulfill other applicable environmental reviews or consultation requirements and what information it needs. In particular, it shall specify any additional information it needs to comment adequately on the draft statement's analysis of significant site-specific effects associated with the granting or approving by that cooperating agency of necessary Federal permits, licenses, or entitlements.

(d) When a cooperating agency with jurisdiction by law objects to or expresses reservations about the proposal on grounds of environmental impacts, the agency expressing the objection or reservation shall specify the mitigation measures it considers necessary to allow the agency to grant or approve applicable permit, license, or related requirements or concurrences.

§ 1503.4 Response to comments.

(a) An agency preparing a final environmental impact statement shall assess and consider comments both individually and collectively, and shall respond by one or more of the means listed below, stating its response in the final statement. Possible responses are to:

(1) Modify alternatives including the proposed action.

(2) Develop and evaluate alternatives not previously given serious consideration by the agency.

(3) Supplement, improve, or modify its analyses.

(4) Make factual corrections.

(5) Explain why the comments do not warrant further agency response, citing the sources, authorities, or reasons which support the agency's position and, if appropriate, indicate those circumstances which would trigger agency reappraisal or further response.

(b) All substantive comments received on the draft statement (or summaries thereof where the response has been exceptionally voluminous), should be attached to the final statement whether or not the comment is thought to merit individual discussion by the agency in the text of the statement.

(c) If changes in response to comments are minor and are confined to the responses described in paragraphs (a)(4) and (5) of this section, agencies may write them on errata sheets and attach them to the statement instead of rewriting the draft statement. In such cases only the comments, the responses, and the changes and not the final statement need be circulated (§ 1502.19). The entire document with a new cover sheet shall be filed as the final statement (§ 1506.9).

PART 1504—PREDECISION REFERRALS TO THE COUNCIL OF PROPOSED FEDERAL ACTIONS DETERMINED TO BE ENVIRONMENTALLY UNSATISFACTORY

Sec.
1504.1   Purpose.
1504.2   Criteria for referral.
1504.3   Procedure for referrals and response.

AUTHORITY: NEPA, the Environmental Quality Improvement Act of 1970, as amended (42 U.S.C. 4371 *et seq.*), sec. 309 of the Clean Air Act, as amended (42 U.S.C. 7609), and E.O. 11514 (Mar. 5, 1970, as amended by E.O. 11991, May 24, 1977).

§ 1504.1 Purpose.

(a) This part establishes procedures for referring to the Council Federal interagency disagreements concerning proposed major Federal actions that might cause unsatisfactory environmental effects. It provides means for early resolution of such disagreements.

(b) Under section 309 of the Clean Air Act (42 U.S.C. 7609), the Administrator of the Environmental Protection Agency is directed to review and comment publicly on the environmental impacts of Federal activities, including actions for which environmental impact statements are prepared. If after this review the Administrator determines that the matter is "unsatisfactory from the standpoint of public health or welfare or environmental quality," section 309 directs that the matter be referred to the Council (hereafter "environmental referrals").

(c) Under section 102(2)(C) of the Act other Federal agencies may make similar reviews of environmental impact statements, including judgments on the acceptability of anticipated environmental impacts. These reviews must be made available to the President, the Council and the public.

[43 FR 55998, Nov. 29, 1978]

§ 1504.2 Criteria for referral.

Environmental referrals should be made to the Council only after concerted, timely (as early as possible in the process), but unsuccessful attempts to resolve differences with the lead agency. In determining what environmental objections to the matter are appropriate to refer to the Council, an agency should weigh potential adverse environmental impacts, considering:

(a) Possible violation of national environmental standards or policies.

(b) Severity.

(c) Geographical scope.

(d) Duration.

(e) Importance as precedents.

(f) Availability of environmentally preferable alternatives.

[43 FR 55998, Nov. 29, 1978]

§ 1504.3 Procedure for referrals and response.

(a) A Federal agency making the referral to the Council shall:

(1) Advise the lead agency at the earliest possible time that it intends to refer a matter to the Council unless a satisfactory agreement is reached.

(2) Include such advice in the referring agency's comments on the draft environmental impact statement, except when the statement does not contain adequate information to permit an assessment of the matter's environmental acceptability.

(3) Identify any essential information that is lacking and request that it be made available at the earliest possible time.

(4) Send copies of such advice to the Council.

(b) The referring agency shall deliver its referral to the Council not later than twenty-five (25) days after the final environmental impact statement has been made available to the Environmental Protection Agency, commenting agencies, and the public. Except when an extension of this period has been granted by the lead agency, the Council will not accept a referral after that date.

(c) The referral shall consist of:

(1) A copy of the letter signed by the head of the referring agency and delivered to the lead agency informing the lead agency of the referral and the reasons for it, and requesting that no action be taken to implement the matter until the Council acts upon the referral. The letter shall include a copy of the statement referred to in (c)(2) of this section.

(2) A statement supported by factual evidence leading to the conclusion that the matter is unsatisfactory from the standpoint of public health or welfare or environmental quality. The statement shall:

(i) Identify any material facts in controversy and incorporate (by reference if appropriate) agreed upon facts,

(ii) Identify any existing environmental requirements or policies which would be violated by the matter,

(iii) Present the reasons why the referring agency believes the matter is environmentally unsatisfactory,

(iv) Contain a finding by the agency whether the issue raised is of national importance because of the threat to national environmental resources or policies or for some other reason,

(v) Review the steps taken by the referring agency to bring its concerns to the attention of the lead agency at the earliest possible time, and

(vi) Give the referring agency's recommendations as to what mitigation alternative, further study, or other course of action (including abandonment of the matter) are necessary to remedy the situation.

(d) Not later than twenty-five (25) days after the referral to the Council the lead agency may deliver a response to the Council, and the referring agency. If the lead agency requests more time and gives assurance that the matter will not go forward in the interim, the Council may grant an extension. The response shall:

(1) Address fully the issues raised in the referral.

(2) Be supported by evidence.

(3) Give the lead agency's response to the referring agency's recommendations.

(e) Interested persons (including the applicant) may deliver their views in writing to the Council. Views in support of the referral should be delivered not later than the referral. Views in support of the response shall be delivered not later than the response.

(f) Not later than twenty-five (25) days after receipt of both the referral and any response or upon being informed that there will be no response (unless the lead agency agrees to a longer time), the Council may take one or more of the following actions:

(1) Conclude that the process of referral and response has successfully resolved the problem.

(2) Initiate discussions with the agencies with the objective of mediation with referring and lead agencies.

(3) Hold public meetings or hearings to obtain additional views and information.

(4) Determine that the issue is not one of national importance and request the referring and lead agencies to pursue their decision process.

(5) Determine that the issue should be further negotiated by the referring and lead agencies and is not appropriate for Council consideration until one or more heads of agencies report to the Council that the agencies' disagreements are irreconcilable.

(6) Publish its findings and recommendations (including where appropriate a finding that the submitted evidence does not support the position of an agency).

(7) When appropriate, submit the referral and the response together with the Council's recommendation to the President for action.

(g) The Council shall take no longer than 60 days to complete the actions specified in paragraph (f)(2), (3), or (5) of this section.

(h) When the referral involves an action required by statute to be determined on the record after opportunity for agency hearing, the referral shall be conducted in a manner consistent with 5 U.S.C. 557(d) (Administrative Procedure Act).

[43 FR 55998, Nov. 29, 1978; 44 FR 873, Jan. 3, 1979]

PART 1505—NEPA AND AGENCY DECISIONMAKING

Sec.

AUTHORITY: NEPA, the Environmental Quality Improvement Act of 1970, as amended (42 U.S.C. 4371 *et seq.*), sec. 309 of the Clean Air Act, as amended (42 U.S.C. 7609), and E.O. 11514 (Mar. 5, 1970, as amended by E.O. 11991, May 24, 1977).

SOURCE: 43 FR 55999, Nov. 29, 1978, unless otherwise noted.

§ 1505.1 Agency decisionmaking procedures.

Agencies shall adopt procedures (§ 1507.3) to ensure that decisions are made in accordance with the policies and purposes of the Act. Such procedures shall include but not be limited to:

(a) Implementing procedures under section 102(2) to achieve the requirements of sections 101 and 102(1).

(b) Designating the major decision points for the agency's principal programs likely to have a significant effect on the human environment and assuring that the NEPA process corresponds with them.

(c) Requiring that relevant environmental documents, comments, and responses be part of the record in formal rulemaking or adjudicatory proceedings.

(d) Requiring that relevant environmental documents, comments, and responses accompany the proposal through existing agency review processes so that agency officials use the statement in making decisions.

(e) Requiring that the alternatives considered by the decisionmaker are encompassed by the range of alternatives discussed in the relevant environmental documents and that the decisionmaker consider the alternatives described in the environmental impact statement. If another decision document accompanies the relevant environmental documents to the decisionmaker, agencies are encouraged to make available to the public before the decision is made any part of that document that relates to the comparison of alternatives.

§1505.2 Record of decision in cases requiring environmental impact statements.

At the time of its decision (§ 1506.10) or, if appropriate, its recommendation to Congress, each agency shall prepare a concise public record of decision. The record, which may be integrated into any other record prepared by the agency, including that required by OMB Circular A-95 (Revised), part I, sections 6(c) and (d), and part II, section 5(b)(4), shall:

(a) State what the decision was.

(b) Identify all alternatives considered by the agency in reaching its decision, specifying the alternative or alternatives which were considered to be environmentally preferable. An agency may discuss preferences among alternatives based on relevant factors including economic and technical considerations and agency statutory missions. An agency shall identify and discuss all such factors including any essential considerations of national policy which were balanced by the agency in making its decision and state how those considerations entered into its decision.

(c) State whether all practicable means to avoid or minimize environmental harm from the alternative selected have been adopted, and if not, why they were not. A monitoring and enforcement program shall be adopted and summarized where applicable for any mitigation.

§ 1505.3 Implementing the decision.

Agencies may provide for monitoring to assure that their decisions are carried out and should do so in important cases. Mitigation (§ 1505.2(c)) and other conditions established in the environmental impact statement or during its review and committed as part of the decision shall be implemented by the lead agency or other appropriate consenting agency. The lead agency shall:

(a) Include appropriate conditions in grants, permits or other approvals.

(b) Condition funding of actions on mitigation.

(c) Upon request, inform cooperating or commenting agencies on progress in carrying out mitigation measures which they have proposed and which were adopted by the agency making the decision.

(d) Upon request, make available to the public the results of relevant monitoring.

PART 1506—OTHER REQUIREMENTS OF NEPA

Sec.

AUTHORITY: NEPA, the Environmental Quality Improvement Act of 1970, as amended (42 U.S.C. 4371 *et seq.*), sec. 309 of the Clean Air Act, as amended (42 U.S.C. 7609), and E.O. 11514 (Mar. 5, 1970, as amended by E.O. 11991, May 24, 1977).

SOURCE: 43 FR 56000, Nov. 29, 1978, unless otherwise noted.

§ 1506.1 Limitations on actions during NEPA process.

(a) Until an agency issues a record of decision as provided in § 1505.2 (except as provided in paragraph (c) of this section), no action concerning the proposal shall be taken which would:

(1) Have an adverse environmental impact; or

(2) Limit the choice of reasonable alternatives.

(b) If any agency is considering an application from a non-Federal entity, and is aware that the applicant is about to take an action within the agency's jurisdiction that would meet either of the criteria in paragraph (a) of this section, then the agency shall promptly notify the applicant that the agency will take appropriate action to insure that the objectives and procedures of NEPA are achieved.

(c) While work on a required program environmental impact statement is in progress and the action is not covered by an existing program statement, agencies shall not undertake in the interim any major Federal action covered by the program which may significantly affect the quality of the human environment unless such action:

(1) Is justified independently of the program;

(2) Is itself accompanied by an adequate environmental impact statement; and

(3) Will not prejudice the ultimate decision on the program. Interim action prejudices the ultimate decision on the program when it tends to determine subsequent development or limit alternatives.

(d) This section does not preclude development by applicants of plans or designs or performance of other work necessary to support an application for Federal, State or local permits or assistance. Nothing in this section shall preclude Rural Electrification Administration approval of minimal expenditures not affecting the environment (*e.g.* long leadtime equipment and purchase options) made by non-governmental entities seeking loan guarantees from the Administration.

§ 1506.2 Elimination of duplication with State and local procedures.

(a) Agencies authorized by law to cooperate with State agencies of statewide jurisdiction pursuant to section 102(2)(D) of the Act may do so.

(b) Agencies shall cooperate with State and local agencies to the fullest extent possible to reduce duplication between NEPA and State and local requirements, unless the agencies are specifically barred from doing so by some other law. Except for cases covered by paragraph (a) of this section, such cooperation shall to the fullest extent possible include:

(1) Joint planning processes.

(2) Joint environmental research and studies.

(3) Joint public hearings (except where otherwise provided by statute).

(4) Joint environmental assessments.

(c) Agencies shall cooperate with State and local agencies to the fullest extent possible to reduce duplication between NEPA and comparable State and local requirements, unless the agencies are specifically barred from doing so by some other law. Except for cases covered by paragraph (a) of this section, such cooperation shall to the fullest extent possible include joint environmental impact statements. In such cases one or more Federal agencies and one or more State or local agencies shall be joint lead agencies. Where State laws or local ordinances have environmental impact statement requirements in addition to but not in conflict with those in NEPA, Federal agencies shall cooperate in fulfilling these requirements as well as those of Federal laws so that one document will comply with all applicable laws.

(d) To better integrate environmental impact statements into State or local planning processes, statements shall discuss any inconsistency of a proposed action with any approved State or local plan and laws (whether or not federally sanctioned). Where an inconsistency exists, the statement should describe the extent to which the agency would reconcile its proposed action with the plan or law.

§ 1506.3 Adoption.

(a) An agency may adopt a Federal draft or final environmental impact statement or portion thereof provided that the statement or portion thereof meets the standards for an adequate statement under these regulations.

(b) If the actions covered by the original environmental impact statement and the proposed action are substantially the same, the agency adopting another agency's statement is not required to recirculate it except as a final statement. Otherwise the adopting agency shall treat the statement as a draft and recirculate it (except as provided in paragraph (c) of this action).

(c) A cooperating agency may adopt without recirculating the environmental impact statement of a lead agency when, after an independent review of the statement, the cooperating agency concludes that its comments and suggestions have been satisfied.

(d) When an agency adopts a statement which is not final within the agency that prepared it, or when the action it assesses is the subject of a referral under part 1504, or when the statement's adequacy is the subject of a judicial action which is not final, the agency shall so specify.

§ 1506.4 Combining documents.

Any environmental document in compliance with NEPA may be combined with any other agency document to reduce duplication and paperwork.

§ 1506.5 Agency responsibility.

(a) *Information.* If an agency requires an applicant to submit environmental information for possible use by the agency in preparing an environmental impact statement, then the agency should assist the applicant by outlining the types of information required. The agency shall independently evaluate the information submitted and shall be responsible for its accuracy. If the agency chooses to use the information submitted by the applicant in the environmental impact statement, either directly or by reference, then the names of the persons responsible for the independent evaluation shall be included in the list of preparers (§ 1502.17). It is the intent of this paragraph that acceptable work not be redone, but that it be verified by the agency.

(b) *Environmental assessments.* If an agency permits an applicant to prepare an environmental assessment, the agency, besides fulfilling the requirements of paragraph (a) of this section, shall make its own evaluation of the environmental issues and take responsibility for the scope and content of the environmental assessment.

(c) *Environmental impact statements.* Except as provided in §§ 1506.2 and 1506.3 any environmental impact statement prepared pursuant to the requirements of NEPA shall be prepared directly by or by a contractor selected by the lead agency or where appropriate under § 1501.6(b), a cooperating agency. It is the intent of these regulations that the contractor be chosen solely by the lead agency, or by the lead agency in cooperation with cooperating agencies, or where appropriate by a cooperating agency to avoid any conflict of interest. Contractors shall execute a disclosure statement prepared by the lead agency, or where appropriate the cooperating agency, specifying that they have no financial or other interest in the outcome of the project. If the document is prepared by contract, the responsible Federal official shall furnish guidance and participate in the preparation and shall independently evaluate the statement prior to its approval and take responsibility for its scope and contents. Nothing in this section is intended to prohibit any agency from requesting any person to submit information to it or to prohibit any person from submitting information to any agency.

§1506.6 Public involvement.

Agencies shall:

(a) Make diligent efforts to involve the public in preparing and implementing their NEPA procedures.

(b) Provide public notice of NEPA-related hearings, public meetings, and the availability of environmental documents so as to inform those persons and agencies who may be interested or affected.

(1) In all cases the agency shall mail notice to those who have requested it on an individual action.

(2) In the case of an action with effects of national concern notice shall include publication in the FEDERAL REGISTER and notice by mail to national organizations reasonably expected to be interested in the matter and may include listing in the *102 Monitor*. An agency engaged in rulemaking may provide notice by mail to national organizations who have requested that notice regularly be provided. Agencies shall maintain a list of such organizations.

(3) In the case of an action with effects primarily of local concern the notice may include:

(i) Notice to State and areawide clearinghouses pursuant to OMB Circular A-95 (Revised).

(ii) Notice to Indian tribes when effects may occur on reservations.

(iii) Following the affected State's public notice procedures for comparable actions.

(iv) Publication in local newspapers (in papers of general circulation rather than legal papers).

(v) Notice through other local media.

(vi) Notice to potentially interested community organizations including small business associations.

(vii) Publication in newsletters that may be expected to reach potentially interested persons.

(viii) Direct mailing to owners and occupants of nearby or affected property.

(ix) Posting of notice on and off site in the area where the action is to be located.

(c) Hold or sponsor public hearings or public meetings whenever appropriate or in accordance with statutory requirements applicable to the agency. Criteria shall include whether there is:

(1) Substantial environmental controversy concerning the proposed action or substantial interest in holding the hearing.

(2) A request for a hearing by another agency with jurisdiction over the action supported by reasons why a hearing will be helpful. If a draft environmental impact statement is to be considered at a public hearing, the agency should make the statement available to the public at least 15 days in advance (unless the purpose of the hearing is to provide information for the draft environmental impact statement).

(d) Solicit appropriate information from the public.

(e) Explain in its procedures where interested persons can get information or status reports on environmental impact statements and other elements of the NEPA process.

(f) Make environmental impact statements, the comments received, and any underlying documents available to the public pursuant to the provisions of the Freedom of Information Act (5 U.S.C. 552), without regard to the exclusion for interagency memoranda where such memoranda transmit comments of Federal agencies on the environmental impact of the proposed action. Materials to be made available to the public shall be provided to the public without charge to the extent practicable, or at a fee which is not more than the actual costs of reproducing copies required to be sent to other Federal agencies, including the Council.

§ 1506.7 Further guidance.

The Council may provide further guidance concerning NEPA and its procedures including:

(a) A handbook which the Council may supplement from time to time which shall in plain language provide guidance and instructions concerning the application of NEPA and these regulations.

(b) Publication of the Council's Memoranda to Heads of Agencies.

(c) In conjunction with the Environmental Protection Agency and the publication of the 102 Monitor, notice of:

(1) Research activities;

(2) Meetings and conferences related to NEPA; and

(3) Successful and innovative procedures used by agencies to implement NEPA.

§ 1506.8 Proposals for legislations.

(a) The NEPA process for proposals for legislation (§ 1508.17) significantly affecting the quality of the human environment shall be integrated with the legislative process of the Congress. A legislative environmental impact statement is the detailed statement required by law to be included in a recommendation or report on a legislative proposal to Congress. A legislative environmental impact statement shall be considered part of the formal transmittal of a legislative proposal to Congress; however, it may be transmitted to Congress up to 30 days later in order to allow time for completion of an accurate statement which can serve as the basis for public and Congressional debate. The statement must be available in time for Congressional hearings and deliberations.

(b) Preparation of a legislative environmental impact statement shall conform to the requirements of these regulations except as follows:

(1) There need not be a scoping process.

(2) The legislative statement shall be prepared in the same manner as a draft statement, but shall be considered the "detailed statement" required by statute; *Provided,* That when any of the following conditions exist both the draft and final environmental impact statement on the legislative proposal shall be prepared and circulated as provided by §§ 1503.1 and 1506.10.

(i) A Congressional Committee with jurisdiction over the proposal has a rule requiring both draft and final environmental impact statements.

(ii) The proposal results from a study process required by statute (such as those required by the Wild and Scenic Rivers Act (16 U.S.C. 1271 *et seq.*) and the Wilderness Act (16 U.S.C. 1131 *et seq.*)).

(iii) Legislative approval is sought for Federal or federally assisted construction or other projects which the agency recommends be located at specific geographic locations. For proposals requiring an environmental impact statement for the acquisition of space by the General Services Administration, a draft statement shall accompany the Prospectus or the 11(b) Report of Building Project Surveys to the Congress, and a final statement shall be completed before site acquisition.

(iv) The agency decides to prepare draft and final statements.

(c) Comments on the legislative statement shall be given to the lead agency which shall forward them along with its own responses to the Congressional committees with jurisdiction.

§ 1506.9 Filing requirements.

Environmental impact statements together with comments and responses shall be filed with the Environmental Protection Agency, attention Office of Federal Activities (A-104), 401 M Street SW., Washington, DC 20460. Statements shall be filed with EPA no earlier than they are also transmitted to commenting agencies and made available to the public. EPA shall deliver one copy of each statement to the Council, which shall satisfy the requirement of availability to the President. EPA may issue guidelines to agencies to implement its responsibilities under this section and § 1506.10.

§ 1506.10 Timing of agency action.

(a) The Environmental Protection Agency shall publish a notice in the *FEDERAL REGISTER* each week of the environmental impact statements filed during the preceding week. The minimum time periods set forth in this section shall be calculated from the date of publication of this notice.

(b) No decision on the proposed action shall be made or recorded under § 1505.2 by a Federal agency until the later of the following dates:

(1) Ninety (90) days after publication of the notice described above in paragraph (a) of this section for a draft environmental impact statement.

(2) Thirty (30) days after publication of the notice described above in paragraph (a) of this section for a final environmental impact statement.

An exception to the rules on timing may be made in the case of an agency decision which is subject to a formal internal appeal. Some agencies have a formally established appeal process which allows other agencies or the public to take appeals on a decision and make their views known, after publication of the final environmental impact statement. In such cases, where a real opportunity exists to alter the decision, the decision may be made and recorded at the same time the environmental impact statement is published. This means that the period for appeal of the decision and the 30-day period prescribed in paragraph (b)(2) of this section may run concurrently. In such cases the environmental impact statement shall explain the timing and the public's right of appeal. An agency engaged in rulemaking under the Administrative Procedure Act or other statute for the purpose of protecting the public health or safety, may waive the time period in paragraph (b)(2) of this section and publish a decision on the final rule simultaneously with publication of the notice of the availability of the final environmental impact statement as described in paragraph (a) of this section.

(c) If the final environmental impact statement is filed within ninety (90) days after a draft environmental impact statement is filed with the Environmental Protection Agency, the minimum thirty (30) day period and the minimum ninety (90) day period may run concurrently. However, subject to paragraph (d) of this section agencies shall allow not less than 45 days for comments on draft statements.

(d) The lead agency may extend prescribed periods. The Environmental Protection Agency may upon a showing by the lead agency of compelling reasons of national policy reduce the prescribed periods and may upon a showing by any other Federal agency of compelling reasons of national policy also extend prescribed periods, but only after consultation with the lead agency. (Also see § 1507.3(d).) Failure to file timely comments shall not be a sufficient reason for extending a period. If the lead agency does not concur with the extension of time, EPA may not extend it for more than 30 days. When the Environmental Protection Agency reduces or extends any period of time it shall notify the Council.

[43 FR 56000, Nov. 29, 1978; 44 FR 874, Jan. 3, 1979]

§ 1506.11 Emergencies.

Where emergency circumstances make it necessary to take an action with significant environmental impact without observing the provisions of these regulations, the Federal agency taking the action should consult with the Council about alternative arrangements. Agencies and the Council will limit such arrangements to actions necessary to control the immediate impacts of the emergency. Other actions remain subject to NEPA review.

§ 1506.12 Effective date.

The effective date of these regulations is July 30, 1979, except that for agencies that administer programs that qualify under section 102(2)(D) of the Act or under section 104(h) of the Housing and Community Development Act of 1974 an additional four months shall be allowed for the State or local agencies to adopt their implementing procedures.

(a) These regulations shall apply to the fullest extent practicable to ongoing activities and environmental documents begun before the effective date. These regulations do not apply to an environmental impact statement or supplement if the draft statement was filed before the effective date of these regulations. No completed environmental documents need be redone by reasons of these regulations. Until these regulations are applicable, the Council's guidelines published in the FEDERAL REGISTER of August 1, 1973, shall continue to be applicable. In cases where these regulations are applicable the guidelines are superseded. However, nothing shall prevent an agency from proceeding under these regulations at an earlier time.

(b) NEPA shall continue to be applicable to actions begun before January 1, 1970, to the fullest extent possible.

PART 1507—AGENCY COMPLIANCE

Sec.

1507.1   Compliance.
1507.2   Agency capability to comply.
1507.3   Agency procedures.

AUTHORITY: NEPA, the Environmental Quality Improvement Act of 1970, as amended (42 U.S.C. 4371 *et seq.*), sec. 309 of the Clean Air Act, as amended (42 U.S.C. 7609), and E.O. 11514 (Mar. 6, 1970, as amended by E.O. 11991, May 24, 1977).

SOURCE: 43 FR 56002, Nov. 29, 1978, unless otherwise noted.

§ 1507.1 Compliance.

All agencies of the Federal Government shall comply with these regulations. It is the intent of these regulations to allow each agency flexibility in adapting its implementing procedures authorized by § 1507.3 to the requirements of other applicable laws.

§ 1507.2 Agency capability to comply.

Each agency shall be capable (in terms of personnel and other resources) of complying with the requirements enumerated below. Such compliance may include use of other's resources, but the using agency shall itself have sufficient capability to evaluate what others do for it. Agencies shall:

(a) Fulfill the requirements of section 102(2)(A) of the Act to utilize a systematic, interdisciplinary approach which will insure the integrated use of the natural and social sciences and the environmental design arts in planning and in decisionmaking which may have an impact on the human environment. Agencies shall designate a person to be responsible for overall review of agency NEPA compliance.

(b) Identify methods and procedures required by section 102(2)(B) to insure that presently unquantified environmental amenities and values may be given appropriate consideration.

(c) Prepare adequate environmental impact statements pursuant to section 102(2)(C) and comment on statements in the areas where the agency has jurisdiction by law or special expertise or is authorized to develop and enforce environmental standards.

(d) Study, develop, and describe alternatives to recommended courses of action in any proposal which involves unresolved conflicts concerning alternative uses of available resources. This requirement of section 102(2)(E) extends to all such proposals, not just the more limited scope of section 102(2)(C)(iii) where the discussion of alternatives is confined to impact statements.

(e) Comply with the requirements of section 102(2)(H) that the agency initiate and utilize ecological information in the planning and development of resource-oriented projects.

(f) Fulfill the requirements of sections 102(2)(F), 102(2)(G), and 102(2)(I), of the Act and of Executive Order 11514, Protection and Enhancement of Environmental Quality, Sec. 2.

§ 1507.3 Agency procedures.

(a) Not later than eight months after publication of these regulations as finally adopted in the FEDERAL REGISTER, or five months after the establishment of an agency, whichever shall come later, each agency shall as necessary adopt procedures to supplement these regulations. When the agency is a department, major subunits are encouraged (with the consent of the department) to adopt their own procedures. Such procedures shall not paraphrase these regulations. They shall confine themselves to implementing procedures. Each agency shall consult with the Council while developing its procedures and before publishing them in the *FEDERAL REGISTER* for comment. Agencies with similar programs should consult with each other and the Council to coordinate their procedures, especially for programs requesting similar information from applicants. The procedures shall be adopted only after an opportunity for public review and after review by the Council for conformity with the Act and these regulations. The Council shall complete its review within 30 days. Once in effect they shall be filed with the Council and made readily available to the public. Agencies are encouraged to publish explanatory guidance for these regulations and their own procedures. Agencies shall continue to review their policies and procedures and in consultation with the Council to revise them as necessary to ensure full compliance with the purposes and provisions of the Act.

(b) Agency procedures shall comply with these regulations except where compliance would be inconsistent with statutory requirements and shall include:

(1) Those procedures required by §§ 1501.2(d), 1502.9(c)(3), 1505.1, 1506.6(e), and 1508.4.

(2) Specific criteria for and identification of those typical classes of action:

(i) Which normally do require environmental impact statements.

(ii) Which normally do not require either an environmental impact statement or an environmental assessment (categorical exclusions (§ 1508.4)).

(iii) Which normally require environmental assessments but not necessarily environmental impact statements.

(c) Agency procedures may include specific criteria for providing limited exceptions to the provisions of these regulations for classified proposals. They are proposed actions which are specifically authorized under criteria established by an Executive Order or statute to be kept secret in the interest of national defense or foreign policy and are in fact properly classified pursuant to such Executive Order or statute. Environmental assessments and environmental impact statements which address classified proposals may be safeguarded and restricted from public dissemination in accordance with agencies' own regulations applicable to classified information. These documents may be organized so that classified portions can be included as annexes, in order that the unclassified portions can be made available to the public.

(d) Agency procedures may provide for periods of time other than those presented in § 1506.10 when necessary to comply with other specific statutory requirements.

(e) Agency procedures may provide that where there is a lengthy period between the agency's decision to prepare an environmental impact statement and the time of actual preparation, the notice of intent required by § 1501.7 may be published at a reasonable time in advance of preparation of the draft statement.

PART 1508—TERMINOLOGY AND INDEX

AUTHORITY: NEPA, the Environmental Quality Improvement Act of 1970, as amended (42 U.S.C. 4371 *et seq.*), sec. 309 of the Clean Air Act, as amended (42 U.S.C. 7609), and E.O. 11514 (Mar. 5, 1970, as amended by E.O. 11991, May 24, 1977).

SOURCE: 43 FR 56003, Nov. 29, 1978, unless otherwise noted.

§ 1508.1 Terminology.

The terminology of this part shall be uniform throughout the Federal Government.

§ 1508.2 Act.

Act means the National Environmental Policy Act, as amended (42 U.S.C. 4321, *et seq.*) which is also referred to as "NEPA."

§ 1508.3 Affecting.

Affecting means will or may have an effect on.

§ 1508.4 Categorical exclusion.

Categorical exclusion means a category of actions which do not individually or cumulatively have a significant effect on the human environment and which have been found to have no such effect in procedures adopted by a Federal agency in implementation of these regulations (§ 1507.3) and for which, therefore, neither an environmental assessment nor an environmental impact statement is required. An agency may decide in its procedures or otherwise, to prepare environmental assessments for the reasons stated in § 1508.9 even though it is not required to do so. Any procedures under this section shall provide for extraordinary circumstances in which a normally excluded action may have a significant environmental effect.

§ 1508.5 Cooperating agency.

Cooperating agency means any Federal agency other than a lead agency which has jurisdiction by law or special expertise with respect to any environmental impact involved in a proposal (or a reasonable alternative) for legislation or other major Federal action significantly affecting the quality of the human environment. The selection and responsibilities of a cooperating agency are described in § 1501.6. A State or local agency of similar qualifications or, when the effects are on a reservation, an Indian Tribe, may by agreement with the lead agency become a cooperating agency.

§ 1508.6 Council.

Council means the Council on Environmental Quality established by title II of the Act.

§ 1508.7 Cumulative impact.

Cumulative impact is the impact on the environment which results from the incremental impact of the action when added to other past, present, and reasonably foreseeable future actions regardless of what agency (Federal or non-Federal) or person undertakes such other actions. Cumulative impacts can result from individually minor but collectively significant actions taking place over a period of time.

§ 1508.8 Effects.

Effects include:

(a) Direct effects, which are caused by the action and occur at the same time and place.

(b) Indirect effects, which are caused by the action and are later in time or farther removed in distance, but are still reasonably foreseeable. Indirect effects may include growth inducing effects and other effects related to induced changes in the pattern of land use, population density or growth rate, and related effects on air and water and other natural systems, including ecosystems. Effects and impacts as used in these regulations are synonymous. Effects includes ecological (such as the effects on natural resources and on the components, structures, and functioning of affected ecosystems), aesthetic, historic, cultural, economic, social, or health, whether direct, indirect, or cumulative. Effects may also include those resulting from actions which may have both beneficial and detrimental effects, even if on balance the agency believes that the effect will be beneficial.

§ 1508.9 Environmental assessment.

Environmental assessment:

(a) Means a concise public document for which a Federal agency is responsible that serves to:

(1) Briefly provide sufficient evidence and analysis for determining whether to prepare an environmental impact statement or a finding of no significant impact.

(2) Aid an agency's compliance with the Act when no environmental impact statement is necessary.

(3) Facilitate preparation of a statement when one is necessary.

(b) Shall include brief discussions of the need for the proposal, of alternatives as required by section 102(2)(E), of the environmental impacts of the proposed action and alternatives, and a listing of agencies and persons consulted.

§ 1508.10 Environmental document.

Environmental document includes the documents specified in § 1508.9 (environmental assessment), § 1508.11 (environmental impact statement), § 1508.13 (finding of no significant impact), and § 1508.22 (notice of intent).

§ 1508.11 Environmental impact statement.

Environmental impact statement means a detailed written statement as required by section 102(2)(C) of the Act.

§ 1508.12 Federal agency.

Federal agency means all agencies of the Federal Government. It does not mean the Congress, the Judiciary, or the President, including the performance of staff functions for the President in his Executive Office. It also includes for purposes of these regulations States and units of general local government and Indian tribes assuming NEPA responsibilities under section 104(h) of the Housing and Community Development Act of 1974.

§ 1508.13 Finding of no significant impact.

Finding of no significant impact means a document by a Federal agency briefly presenting the reasons why an action, not otherwise excluded (§ 1508.4), will not have a significant effect on the human environment and for which an environmental impact statement therefore will not be prepared. It shall include the environmental assessment or a summary of it and shall note any other environmental documents related to it (§ 1501.7(a)(5)). If the assessment is included, the finding need not repeat any of the discussion in the assessment but may incorporate it by reference.

§ 1508.14 Human environment.

Human environment shall be interpreted comprehensively to include the natural and physical environment and the relationship of people with that environment. (See the definition of "effects" (§ 1508.8).) This means that economic or social effects are not intended by themselves to require preparation of an environmental impact statement. When an environmental impact statement is prepared and economic or social and natural or physical environmental effects are interrelated, then the environmental impact statement will discuss all of these effects on the human environment.

§ 1508.15 Jurisdiction by law.

Jurisdiction by law means agency authority to approve, veto, or finance all or part of the proposal.

§ 1508.16 Lead agency.

Lead agency means the agency or agencies preparing or having taken primary responsibility for preparing the environmental impact statement.

§ 1508.17 Legislation.

Legislation includes a bill or legislative proposal to Congress developed by or with the significant cooperation and support of a Federal agency, but does not include requests for appropriations. The test for significant cooperation is whether the proposal is in fact predominantly that of the agency rather than another source. Drafting does not by itself constitute significant cooperation. Proposals for legislation include requests for ratification of treaties. Only the agency which has primary responsibility for the subject matter involved will prepare a legislative environmental impact statement.

§ 1508.18 Major Federal action.

Major Federal action includes actions with effects that may be major and which are potentially subject to Federal control and responsibility. Major reinforces but does not have a meaning independent of significantly (§ 1508.27). Actions include the circumstance where the responsible officials fail to act and that failure to act is reviewable by courts or administrative tribunals under the Administrative Procedure Act or other applicable law as agency action.

(a) Actions include new and continuing activities, including projects and programs entirely or partly financed, assisted, conducted, regulated, or approved by federal agencies; new or revised agency rules, regulations, plans, policies. or procedures; and legislative proposals (§§ 1506.8, 1508.17). Actions do not include funding assistance solely in the form of general revenue sharing funds distributed under the State and Local Fiscal Assistance Act of 1972, 31 U.S.C. 1221 *et seq.*, with no Federal agency control over the subsequent use of such funds. Actions do not include bringing judicial or administrative civil or criminal enforcement actions.

(b) Federal actions tend to fall within one of the following categories:

(1) Adoption of official policy, such as rules, regulations, and interpretations adopted pursuant to the Administrative Procedure Act, 5 U.S.C. 551 *et seq.*; treaties and international conventions or agreements; formal documents establishing an agency's policies which will result in or substantially alter agency programs.

(2) Adoption of formal plans, such as official documents prepared or approved by federal agencies which guide or prescribe alternative uses of Federal resources, upon which future agency actions will be based.

(3) Adoption of programs, such as a group of concerted actions to implement a specific policy or plan; systematic and connected agency decisions allocating agency resources to implement a specific statutory program or executive directive.

(4) Approval of specific projects, such as construction or management activities located in a defined geographic area. Projects include actions approved by permit or other regulatory decision as well as federal and federally assisted activities.

§ 1508.19 Matter.

Matter includes for purposes of part 1504:

(a) With respect to the Environmental Protection Agency, any proposed legislation, project, action or regulation as those terms are used in section 309(a) of the Clean Air Act (42 U.S.C. 7609).

(b) With respect to all other agencies, any proposed major federal action to which section 102(2)(C) of NEPA applies.

§ 1508.20 Mitigation.

Mitigation includes:

(a) Avoiding the impact altogether by not taking a certain action or parts of an action.

(b) Minimizing impacts by limiting the degree or magnitude of the action and its implementation.

(c) Rectifying the impact by repairing, rehabilitating, or restoring the affected environment.

(d) Reducing or eliminating the impact over time by preservation and maintenance operations during the life of the action.

(e) Compensating for the impact by replacing or providing substitute resources or environments.

§ 1508.21 NEPA process.

NEPA process means all measures necessary for compliance with the requirements of section 2 and title I of NEPA.

§ 1508.22 Notice of intent.

Notice of intent means a notice that an environmental impact statement will be prepared and considered. The notice shall briefly:

(a) Describe the proposed action and possible alternatives.

(b) Describe the agency's proposed scoping process including whether, when, and where any scoping meeting will be held.

(c) State the name and address of a person within the agency who can answer questions about the proposed action and the environmental impact statement.

§ 1508.23 Proposal.

Proposal exists at that stage in the development of an action when an agency subject to the Act has a goal and is actively preparing to make a decision on one or more alternative means of accomplishing that goal and the effects can be meaningfully evaluated. Preparation of an environmental impact statement on a proposal should be timed (§ 1502.5) so that the final statement may be completed in time for the statement to be included in any recommendation or report on the proposal. A proposal may exist in fact as well as by agency declaration that one exists.

§ 1508.24 Referring agency.

Referring agency means the federal agency which has referred any matter to the Council after a determination that the matter is unsatisfactory from the standpoint of public health or welfare or environmental quality.

§ 1508.25 Scope.

Scope consists of the range of actions, alternatives, and impacts to be considered in an environmental impact statement. The scope of an individual statement may depend on its relationships to other statements (§§ 1502.20 and 1508.28). To determine the scope of environmental impact statements, agencies shall consider 3 types of actions, 3 types of alternatives, and 3 types of impacts. They include:

(a) Actions (other than unconnected single actions) which may be:

(1) Connected actions, which means that they are closely related and therefore should be discussed in the same impact statement. Actions are connected if they:

(i) Automatically trigger other actions which may require environmental impact statements.

(ii) Cannot or will not proceed unless other actions are taken previously or simultaneously.

(iii) Are interdependent parts of a larger action and depend on the larger action for their justification.

(2) Cumulative actions, which when viewed with other proposed actions have cumulatively significant impacts and should therefore be discussed in the same impact statement.

(3) Similar actions, which when viewed with other reasonably foreseeable or proposed agency actions, have similarities that provide a basis for evaluating their environmental consequences together, such as common timing or geography. An agency may wish to analyze these actions in the same impact statement. It should do so when the best way to assess adequately the combined impacts of similar actions or reasonable alternatives to such actions is to treat them in a single impact statement.

(b) Alternatives which include: (1) No action alternative.

(2) Other reasonable courses of actions.

(3) Mitigation measures (not in the proposed action).

(c) Impacts, which may be: (1) Direct; (2) indirect; (3) cumulative.

§ 1508.26 Special expertise.

Special expertise means statutory responsibility, agency mission, or related program experience.

§ 1508.27 Significantly.

Significantly as used in NEPA requires considerations of both context and intensity:

(a) *Context.* This means that the significance of an action must be analyzed in several contexts such as society as a whole (human, national), the affected region, the affected interests, and the locality. Significance varies with the setting of the proposed action. For instance, in the case of a site-specific action, significance would usually depend upon the effects in the locale rather than in the world as a whole. Both short- and long-term effects are relevant.

(b) *Intensity.* This refers to the severity of impact. Responsible officials must bear in mind that more than one agency may make decisions about partial aspects of a major action. The following should be considered in evaluating intensity:

(1) Impacts that may be both beneficial and adverse. A significant effect may exist even if the Federal agency believes that on balance the effect will be beneficial.

(2) The degree to which the proposed action affects public health or safety.

(3) Unique characteristics of the geographic area such as proximity to historic or cultural resources, park lands, prime farmlands, wetlands, wild and scenic rivers, or ecologically critical areas.

(4) The degree to which the effects on the quality of the human environment are likely to be highly controversial.

(5) The degree to which the possible effects on the human environment are highly uncertain or involve unique or unknown risks.

(6) The degree to which the action may establish a precedent for future actions with significant effects or represents a decision in principle about a future consideration.

(7) Whether the action is related to other actions with individually insignificant but cumulatively significant impacts. Significance exists if it is reasonable to anticipate a cumulatively significant impact on the environment. Significance cannot be avoided by terming an action temporary or by breaking it down into small component parts.

(8) The degree to which the action may adversely affect districts, sites, highways, structures, or objects listed in or eligible for listing in the National Register of Historic Places or may cause loss or destruction of significant scientific, cultural, or historical resources.

(9) The degree to which the action may adversely affect an endangered or threatened species or its habitat that has been determined to be critical under the Endangered Species Act of 1973.

(10) Whether the action threatens a violation of Federal, State, or local law or requirements imposed for the protection of the environment.

[43 FR 56003, Nov. 29, 1978; 44 FR 874, Jan. 3, 1979]

§ 1508.28 Tiering.

Tiering refers to the coverage of general matters in broader environmental impact statements (such as national program or policy statements) with subsequent narrower statements or environmental analyses (such as regional or basinwide program statements or ultimately site-specific statements) incorporating by reference the general discussions and concentrating solely on the issues specific to the statement subsequently prepared. Tiering is appropriate when the sequence of statements or analyses is:

(a) From a program, plan, or policy environmental impact statement to a program, plan, or policy statement or analysis of lesser scope or to a site-specific statement or analysis.

(b) From an environmental impact statement on a specific action at an early stage (such as need and site selection) to a supplement (which is preferred) or a subsequent statement or analysis at a later stage (such as environmental mitigation). Tiering in such cases is appropriate when it helps the lead agency to focus on the issues which are ripe for decision and exclude from consideration issues already decided or not yet ripe.

Index to Parts 1500 Through 1508

EDITORIAL NOTE: This listing is provided for information purposes only. It is compiled and kept up-to-date by the Council on Environmental Quality.

Index